Camp, Car Washes, Heaven, and Hell...

Published by Bethany House Publishers
A Ministry of Bethany Fellowship, Inc.
11300 Hampshire Avenue South
Minneapolis, Minnesota 55438

Printed in the United States of America.

Library of Congress Cataloging-in-Publication Data

Shellenberger, Susie.
   Camp, carwashes, heaven, and hell / Susie Shellenberger and Greg Johnson.
      p. cm. — (77 pretty important ideas on living God's way)
   Summary: Short readings discuss the value of talkiing to God on a regular basis,
the importance of having the Bible as an authoritative guide, and other aspects of
Christian life.
   ISBN 1-55661-484-5
   1. Teenagers—Religious life. 2. Christian life—Juvenile literature.
Yl. Christian life. 2. Prayer books and devotions."
I. Johnson, Greg. II. Title. III. Series: Shellenberger, Susie. 77 pretty important
ideas.
BV4531.2.S46   1996
248.8'3—dc20
                                    96-10057
                                     CIP
                                     AC

Camp, Car Washes, Heaven, and Hell...

▼ ▼ ▼ ▼ ▼ ▼ ▼ ▼ ▼

SUSIE SHELLENBERGER
& GREG JOHNSON

BETHANY HOUSE PUBLISHERS
MINNEAPOLIS, MINNESOTA 55438

77 Pretty Important Ideas

Lockers, Lunchlines, Chemistry, and Cliques
Cars, Curfews, Parties, and Parents
Camp, Car Washes, Heaven, and Hell
Life, Love, Music, and Money

Dedicated to

Mercy Eyadiel and Juli Tolle

Thanks for being students who made English and speech classes a fun memory. You taught this ex-teacher some valuable insights through your questions, your dreams, and your lives. I'm still waiting, however, for your essay on Thoreau.

I'm proud of you.
—Susie Shellenberger

SUSIE SHELLENBERGER is the editor of *Brio* magazine for teen girls (cir. 160,000), published by FOCUS ON THE FAMILY. A graduate of SOUTHERN NAZARENE UNIVERSITY and the UNIVERSITY OF CENTRAL OKLAHOMA, Susie's experience with teens ranges from youth ministry to teaching high school speech and drama. She is the author of nine books, including *There's a Sheep in My Mirror* and *Straight Ahead*.

GREG JOHNSON is the former editor of *Breakaway* magazine for teen boys (cir. 90,000) and the author or coauthor of fifteen books, including *If I Could Ask God One Question* and *Daddy's Home*. A graduate of NORTHWEST CHRISTIAN COLLEGE, Greg has been involved with teens for over fifteen years and has worked with YOUTH FOR CHRIST and FOCUS ON THE FAMILY. He and his wife have two sons and make their home in Colorado Springs, where Greg is a literary agent for ALIVE COMMUNICATIONS.

Churches are FULL of imperfect people.

No, you may not see a lot of physically disabled people in church, but you will see a lot of emotionally or spiritually disabled. Of course, you can't really tell who they are. **A lot of them look quite normal.** True, there are some who DO look kind of funny on the outside—many are older, some a bit more wrinkled . . . and a few still wear polyester. But if that trips you up and keeps you from church, well, let's just say it isn't CHURCH people who have the problem. It's *you!*

Church members are simply saved sinners. Some are still struggling with sin that's easily noticed, but most have learned to hide their sins—especially at church functions. But they all have one thing in common: Even if they can hide their exterior imperfections from *you*, they can't hide their interior imperfections from God.

That fact puts us all on a level playing field . . . but **there's one pretty cool difference.** When God looks at all this massive imperfection from those who have truly trusted Jesus Christ to save them from their sins, all He chooses to see is Jesus. He doesn't see the mistakes—and doesn't give a rip about wrinkles or polyester!

Unfortunately, when some people look at all of the less-than-perfect people, they say, "Get me outta here!" They just see the hypocrisy—or maybe the polyester—and decide **they can't handle that much imperfection.**

Next time you notice that people aren't so perfect, try doing what God does: Look at the Jesus in them instead, and notice their effort (hey, at least they're in church!). And if they don't have Jesus, pray that they soon will.

PRAY every day. You'll be amazed at what happens.

Seriously. If you want a close relationship with your heavenly Father, it only makes sense to talk with Him daily. **It doesn't feel good when one of your best friends ignores you, does it?** Imagine how God feels when you try to go through the day without Him.

When you realize the incredible power that's available to you through prayer, you'll *anticipate* having conversations with Him.

Several years ago a widowed Mexican woman with two children had come to the end of her resources—literally. She only had 22 cents! But she was a godly woman and knew where to turn for guidance. She spent *three hours* in prayer, asking God what to do. She sensed He was telling her to go to El Dorado, a huge market in a nearby city. She obediently got up and made the trip.

When she arrived, she sensed the Lord telling her to grab a grocery cart and fill it with three months' worth of groceries—the essentials—items she and her two children really needed. She obeyed and carefully selected the supplies.

Finished shopping, she headed toward the checkout lines. This particular market was so big, it had 120 different lanes! **She was over-whelmed** . . . but she had spent three hours in prayer. As she neared the front of the store, she strongly felt God leading her to checkout lane number seven. There was only one man in front of her.

When the clerk had finished checking him out, she stepped outside her counter and pulled the closed chain across the aisle. "Sorry," she said. "You'll have to find another lane. It's my lunch break."

The little widow gently looked into the eyes of the young clerk and quietly said, "No. My Father told me to come here. I'll wait." The clerk shrugged her shoulders, smacked her gum, and left.

An hour later she returned to find the widow standing in exactly the same spot—right outside the chain of checkout lane number seven. The clerk rolled her eyes, unfastened the chain, and motioned for the woman to push her cart forward.

As each item was being registered, the widow fingered the 22 cents in her purse. Only two items left in her cart. **What will I do?** she wondered. Yet she remained calm, knowing she was acting in obedience to her heavenly Father.

As the clerk was ringing up the last item in her cart, a voice came on over the loudspeaker. "Congratulations, shoppers!" welcomed the manager. "Today is the seventh anniversary of El Dorado Market. Whoever is standing in checkout lane number seven being checked out *right now* will receive everything on the house!"

When I (Susie) first heard this story shared by a missionary, my first reaction was "YES, YES, YES!" But as I thought about it, I realized that's exactly the kind of ending I *should* have expected. After all, **doesn't God promise to meet all our needs?** Remember the sparrows and lilies?

"Don't worry about *things*—food, drink, and clothes. For you already have life and a body—and they are far more important than what to eat and wear. Look at the birds! They don't worry about what to eat—they don't need to sow or reap or store up food—for your heavenly Father feeds them. And you are far more valuable to him than they are. Will all your worries add a single moment to your life?

"And why worry about your clothes? Look at the field lilies! They don't worry about theirs. Yet King Solomon in all his glory was not clothed as beautifully as they. And **if God cares** so wonderfully for flowers that are here today and gone tomorrow, won't he more surely care for you, O men of little faith?" (Matthew 6:25–30, TLB).

The Old Testament reminds us just how intently He's watching our lives: "For the eyes of the LORD range throughout the earth to strengthen those whose hearts are fully committed to him" (2 Chronicles 16:9a, NIV).

Those eyes are not the eyes of a traffic-cop God, just waiting to write us up for something we've done wrong. Those are the eyes of a loving, giving Father who's just looking for an opportunity to jump into *your* life during *your* day and lift *your* load. He *wants* to make your day a better one! But you'll never know how much He has to offer unless you spend time talking with Him every single day.

So develop a strong prayer life. Everything in your life will make more sense if you do. **Promise.**

God wants to be your BEST friend.

But He also wants to be your Savior,

your **Guide,**

your Counselor,

your Redeemer,

your Physician,

your Shelter,

your God.

So let Him be all He wants to be in your life.

4 } Your life SCREAMS a lot louder than your words.

We know. We know. You *want* to tell others about Christ, but you're tongue-tied, or you're scared, or you just plain don't know what to say. (Try to get your hands on a copy of *Keeping Your Cool While Sharing Your Faith* by Greg Johnson and Susie Shellenberger, Tyndale House Publishers.) Meanwhile, know that **your actions carry a LOT of weight**—sometimes even more than your words.

Here, we'll show you what we mean. In each example, check which one would mean MORE to you:

1. Your dad just lost his job.

_____ Christian Mary says, "I'll pray for you."

_____ Christian Terry brings a bucket of the Colonel's chicken to your house around 5 P.M.

2. You took a mean fall at basketball practice and broke your ankle.

_____ Christian Mary calls and says, "If you need anything, let me know, OK?"

_____ Christian Terry comes by after school bringing your homework and study guides and offers to help you catch up during the next week.

Camp, Car Washes, Heaven, and Hell • 15

3. Your dad got a new job in another city. Your family doesn't know *anyone*.

Naturally, you're a little nervous during

your first day as the new kid in school.

_____ Christian Mary sits across from you in math class and says, "We've

got a great youth group. Bible study is tomorrow night at 7 P.M.

Hope to see you there!"

_____ Christian Terry sits across from you in history. "Can I pick you up

for Bible study tomorrow night?"

Both genuinely cared. But Terry's efforts were always backed with *action*.

Words are important, but actions are remembered a lot longer.

One HOUR of worship a week isn't enough.

Sometimes when you're singing in church, it takes two or three songs before you start to actually pay attention to what the lyrics are saying. That's because **your mind is on other things** (lunch, breakfast, the opposite sex, sports, the opposite sex, plowing the back forty). In fact, you might be nearly done singing before your mind tunes in to what you're supposed to be doing—taking your mind off of yourself and focusing on worshiping God for being who He is. Total worship time? About five minutes. Guess what? That's not enough!

We've discovered a few ways to get more out of Sunday worship time, whether it involves music or drama or prayer or another form of worship:

• Before you head off to church, listen to some music that pulls your thoughts in the right direction.

• **Take some time with God** BEFORE the service, and don't think that going to church covers your one-on-one time with God for the day.

• As the service begins, **ask God to clear your mind** of things that would distract you from recognizing how wonderful He is. (This is good to do anytime. Satan just likes to get our minds on other things besides worship.)

• Most of all, keep in mind that worship is not just a Sunday thing.

Look at the quick definition again: When can you take your mind off of yourself and put it on God and Jesus? Anytime, right?! So when you notice something in God's creation that's awe-inspiring; when you take time to serve another human being in some way; when you give something you've called yours to the Lord; when you say in your heart, *God, thanks for allowing me to live another day on this earth*, or *Thanks for giving me great parents, good friends, a warm bed, food, clothes, etc.*, you're actually worshiping. **The more you do it, the more exciting it gets.** Worship is good.

Never underestimate the POWER of your heavenly Father.

- He made a *donkey* talk, remember?

- He invented color and rhyme and the Grand Canyon and Niagara Falls.

- He knows how the tide is born and where the waves are stored.

- **He gives great gifts!** Take peace, for instance: "I am leaving you with a gift—peace of mind and heart! And the peace I give isn't fragile like the peace the world gives. So don't be troubled or afraid" (John 14:27, TLB).

- He can make a human being from a teeny, tiny sperm and a teeny, tiny egg. What's even *more* amazing is the fact that it all started with a dirt clod!

- He knows the exact number of hairs on your head.

- He can make a hyena laugh.

- **His fruit wears well.** (Love, joy, peace, patience, kindness, goodness, faithfulness, gentleness, and self-control. For more info on His fruit, see Galatians 5:22–23.)

- He calls stars by name . . . in galaxies mankind hasn't even discovered yet.

- He saw you way back when you were being *conceived!*

- **He has your fingerprints memorized.**

- He created the hop and spring in the legs of kangaroos.

- He determines how far the waves roll and with what strength.

- He's the author of intuition and instinct.

- He understands the wildness in each animal He designed to live on earth.

- He tells daylight how far to spread her wings of illumination.

- He balances the clouds with exact perfection and skill.

- He used *music* to knock down walls!

- He offered a fish buffet for thousands . . . from one small sack lunch.

- Though you don't deserve it, **He's crazy with love for you.**

Know WHY the Bible was written.

Do you ever wonder why we have to have a Bible to read and obey? Why can't we just follow our feelings or our conscience—or maybe what our friends say is right and wrong about life and God?

The purpose of the Bible isn't only to give us a moral road map to follow, but if you think about it, **this is hugely important.** If an authoritative guide weren't available, people WOULD do whatever they felt like doing. And though you might think it'd be cool to do what YOU feel like doing, it DEFINITELY wouldn't be cool to let others do what they feel like doing to YOU! (FYI: This includes the people who are currently in prison.)

If we tried to keep order in society just by letting everyone follow their conscience, it wouldn't be any better than people always doing what they feel like doing. Here's why: Once you do something your conscience tells you is wrong, then do it again, and do it again . . . pretty soon your conscience isn't talking to you anymore. You've trained yourself to ignore it; you've buried it, and it can't function like it was supposed to. **Take cheating for example.** You probably can't even remember the first time you let your eyes drift to a classmate's paper during a test. Since you probably got away with it and didn't get caught or punished, your conscience may not have bugged you too much. That's how people get started making a habit of cheating on their homework. *No consequences, no problem,* they think. Their consciences have been effectively neutralized!

The same thing happens with alcohol, drugs, lying, or going too far sexually. **The more you step over the line your**

conscience has drawn, the easier it gets.

So, do you see why people have used the Bible as a moral guide? In fact, most of our laws came out of the Bible.

But **God didn't give us the Bible just so we would have some good rules to live by.**

The biggest reason for the Bible is to show us what HE is like and reveal to us what is most important in life.

Also know that not EVERY word in the Bible will apply to your life today.

The Bible is like the last letter a father writes to much-loved children who he won't see face-to-face for a loooooooooong time. God carefully chose words of instruction and the most important points about family history. True, **all of that history and stuff doesn't always seem to apply to you now** . . . but you've got to realize that the Bible wasn't just written for you to survive junior and senior high school. It was carefully crafted to help people through the centuries get the most out of their ENTIRE lives. And you're not just going to need its wisdom and comfort while you're a teenager; you're going to need it when you're seventy years old, too.

That type of goal—being everything to everyone for their whole life—is BIG. Maybe that's why there are so many pages.

So the next time you're wondering, *Why this BIG Book?* or you're thinking, *The Bible doesn't apply to MY life,* just remember that not only was it given to our ancestors for all of their todays, and to all of our children and grandchildren for their todays, but it was also given to YOU for today. No wonder it's a big book!

Last point: **The Bible is the perfect guide** to help you truly understand God's character. **But you've got to read the whole thing** to GET His whole character. You can't judge God by the wars in the Old Testament without looking at the cross in the New Testament. That would be like reading half of your science book and saying you completely understand science. How could you when you've only read half the book?

A Christian leader you TRUST will fail you.

A Sunday school teacher who is really good . . . will up and quit without telling anyone why.

A youth leader whom you think you know better than anyone . . . will leave his wife and go live with someone else.

A pastor will start drinking heavily . . . and be forced out of the church.

A TV preacher or well-known Christian musician . . . will be involved in some sort of scandal, thereby falling off of a pedestal that probably shouldn't have been there in the first place.

And you'll be left wondering, *If Christ and Christianity is so real and so important,* **why can't the people I trust keep their lives in order?** *If THEY can't keep on the narrow road, how could I ever hope to?*

We don't know what lesson number it is, but this one is essential: **Christian leaders are fallible,** just like you and your friends. They're going to mess up small-time, and they're going to mess up BIG-TIME! It'll feel rotten when one of YOUR leaders messes up, **but that doesn't change who God is,** what Jesus did, or the Holy Spirit's ability to empower you not to fall into the same traps your leaders did.

In short: It's foolish to walk away from church or turn your back on God because someone else did . . . even if that someone was someone you trusted.

But just because one does, that doesn't mean they ALL will.

Nearly all of your shepherds and leaders will be wonderful. Oh sure, you'll see them make mistakes, but most won't be too bad. By their lives (and sometimes their words), they'll point you down that narrow road. And though you'll see how tough it is to follow that path, you'll want to because of their example. They'll demonstrate how you can avoid the potholes and sharp curves with no guardrails. When you DO stumble over something and fall flat on your face, they'll be there to pick you up, dust you off, and tell you it's OK—that **God forgives every major and minor stumble,** and that **all He wants is for you to keep pressing forward.**

That's when you'll **thank God He's given you a leader to follow.** You won't thank Him for making your leader perfect (ain't no such thing, remember), but you'll thank Him for this helpful companion and guide on the path to LIFE.

God wants to TRANSFORM you.

He's not just interested in helping you look like you have your act together. **Anyone can look good** on the *outside*. But guess what? It's the *inside* that counts.

God wants to clean you up deep down—where your soul is. He doesn't want to settle for just hearing you talk to Him every day. He wants to be Lord of your life. In other words, He wants to *reign*. To live in and through every fiber of your being. To possess your thinking and fill you with His power.

How does this happen? **You have to consciously choose it.**

Jesus, save me from myself. Forgive me for my self-centeredness. I choose to follow your lead. Take complete control.

Now that you've consciously chosen it, **start living it.**

God isn't PUNISHING people by sending earthquakes and Ebola.

Earthquakes in San Francisco and Los Angeles.

Typhoons that kill 100,000 in India.

Floods in China.

Measles in Angola.

Hurricanes in Florida.

Blizzards in North Dakota.

Typhoid in the Amazon.

The question that you'll hear debated at school or when you hit the work world is, **Does God make natural disasters and disease happen because He's ticked off** and wants to kill a lot of people at once?

That's a huge question with only one simple answer:

No.

Any Christian who would say "yes" to that question is trying to speak for God when he or she really doesn't have a clue.

True, God used an earthquake to swallow 3,000 rebellious and idol-worshiping Israelites (see Exodus 32), but that was an exception, not the rule. **The Bible doesn't say that** whenever dangerous natural events or diseases occur that **God is mad** and trying to punish people.

The polio epidemic in the early part of this century crippled hundreds of thousands of people—mostly children—before a cure was discovered. Was God mad at kids and simply found a way to punish helpless little children?

Measles, smallpox, chicken pox, mumps, and other diseases that used to kill thousands each year are now nearly eradicated from North America . . . but not the rest of the world. Is God happy with Americans and Canadians but angry at Africans and those who live in South America?

Do you see the dilemma in asserting that God is intentionally causing every disease, accident, or weather condition that kills or maims someone?

Living God's way means representing God in an accurate way.

Victorious Christian living DOESN'T mean what you think.

A victorious Christian . . .

always smiles;

never has problems;

has every prayer answered;

leads all of her friends to Christ;

never gets mad or irritated with others;

understands everything he reads in the Bible.

If these were the criteria for living like a victorious Christian, the answer would be, A victorious Christian . . . *doesn't exist!*

Don't get fooled by someone else's definition of what a Christian should look like or how a Christian should feel or what a Christian should do. If you do buy in to another's standards, you'll also buy in to a lot of frustration and depression.

Here are the big questions with obvious answers:

•Did Jesus Christ die on a cross to take away the penalty of your sin?

•Does He promise abundant life on this earth and eternal life in heaven for faithful followers?

•Does the Bible ever communicate that God's love for you today is conditioned on how well you "perform" for Him?

Is the picture clear? You ALREADY HAVE the victory because of what Christ has done. You have been promised access to the Father through Christ. He has promised to care for all of your needs (not your greeds). **He loves you unconditionally**— good performance or not.

So, are you a victorious Christian?

God WANTS to use you.

He's given you special gifts and abilities that He wants to use to impact those around you. In other words, **He wants to use you the way He created you.** If you're not an "up-front" person, He's probably not going to ask you to stand in front of the student body and quote Scripture. If, however, you hate being behind the scenes and like more action, He probably *will* use you up front. (Maybe not to quote Scripture, but possibly to run for office and be a student leader. This is a terrific way to make a difference in the atmosphere at your school.)

What if I don't know what my special gifts are?

That's a good question, and we're glad you asked. Sometimes it takes a while to discover the specific gifts God *has* blessed us with. It may take some growing. The older you get—and the more things you become involved with—the better God can help you discern that.

If you're still in the process of discovering what your gifts are, don't let that slow you down from being used by God. **Give what you have right now**—your very *self*! **You'll be amazed at what God can do with a life that's completely His.**

Many Christians win the battle but lose the war. DON'T be one of them.

When discussing the Bible, God, or your personal beliefs with someone who disagrees, you can—with enough persistence, arguing, and shrewd conniving—finally get your point across. But what good is *that* if you've lost your effectiveness to later lead that person to Christ?

Choose your battles carefully. Some things just aren't worth fighting over.

GARBAGE In. Garbage Out.

It's true that whatever we put into our minds will eventually come out through our lifestyle. Whatever is on the inside will sooner or later show up on the outside.

Check out what Proverbs 4:23 says: "Be careful how you think; your life is shaped by your thoughts" (GNB).

What influences your thoughts? The movies you see, the TV shows you watch, the music you listen to, the books and magazines you read, the conversations you soak up.

Jesus tells us that we'll know a tree by its fruit. In other words, a tree with cherries on it is pretty certain to be a cherry tree. Likewise, a person who consistently, and **without remorse, cusses, cheats, gossips,** and goes too far with a boyfriend/girlfriend probably isn't a Christian. The fruit doesn't match up. Christians grow good fruit: kindness, goodness, love, and a bunch more.

What kind of fruit do others see in *your* life? Hmmm. Guess that's determined by what kind of STUFF you're allowing into your mind.

Be careful. **Be really, really, really careful!**

It IS important to memorize Scripture.

When you were little and you were about to cross the street, what did your mom say? You can still hear it, can't you? "Take my hand" or "Look both ways." She said it every time.

Now those words are a part of you, and **you're still careful when you cross the street** because of your mom's repetition. The same goes for memorizing God's Word. It'll come to be a part of every choice you make.

Do you know what God says about your anger or mouth getting out of control?

What kind of giver does God like?

What should you do without ceasing?

What did Jesus say about forgiveness when He was hanging on the cross?

Why should you honor your father and mother?

If you had memorized Proverbs 18:21, 2 Corinthians 9:7, 1 Thessalonians 5:17, Luke 23:34, and Ephesians 6:3, **you'd know the answers** almost without thinking about it.

We're going to assume you're not like those teens who don't want to listen to anyone else. (If you were, you probably wouldn't be reading this book.) And we're going to assume you realize getting advice from God is just about the most important thing you can do.

That's why **memorizing God's Word is so essential.** If you want to hear His voice automatically when a situation or question arises, the best way is to have it hidden in your heart and mind. Take the one-verse-a-week challenge for a month. Just four verses—that's all we ask. If you need some suggestions, ask your folks or youth leader. Write each verse out on a 3 x 5 card, and look at it several times a day. Consistently review verses you've memorized, and you'll soon be able to hear God's voice consistently. **He speaks to you through His Word,** but He doesn't just want to speak when you're reading the Bible; **He wants you to hear His voice all day long.**

18. Stay PLUGGED Into the Power!

The same power that raised a dead man to life . . . and hung the stars in the sky . . . and set the world in motion . . . is yours to claim and live your life by on a daily basis.

If you're committed 100 percent to Jesus Christ, *you* have that power inside YOU! So, **let's do a power check.** Is your power lying dormant inside your heart? Or has it splashed out into your lifestyle?

Here's the secret for *living* in God's power:

Live His letter. The Bible is God's personal letter to *you*. It's jam-packed with instruction, advice, and wisdom. It keeps you plugged into His plan for your life.

But don't stop with simply *reading* this letter. Determine to *live* it! **Put His words into practice.** Adopt the Bible as part of your very lifestyle. Read it and apply it—every single day.

Connect your cable. Your HEART acts as a cable. Make sure you stay intimately connected to Jesus Christ. Why? Because He's your main power source. How do you *stay* connected? By reading your Bible every day and through developing a consistent prayer life.

Prayer is simply talking to God and listening for His response. It's through your daily prayer time that God reveals important things to you: stuff like how to impact those around you, who to reach out to at school, areas in your life that need working on, and staying connected to Him. If you have any loose wires, He'll illuminate that area so you can tighten the cable and **maintain a strong connection to the Power Source.**

You can fool all of the people some of the time. And you can fool some of the people all of the time. But guess what? You CAN'T fool God any of the time.

So don't even think about being a phony.

God doesn't NEED to use you; He wants to use you.

If God is all-powerful, all-knowing, all-everywhere . . . all-everything, why would He choose to work through people as His major way of reaching the world? After all, He could use the clouds to write out everything He wants done.

He could perform incredible miracles of healing and sign His name in disappearing ink across the arms of those He healed to prove He did it. He could drop millions of sandwiches on the hungry without ever coming close to emptying the heavenly fridge—and could even include a signed gospel tract in each one so they'd know the Source.

He could do all that and more.

But instead, He's decided the best way to reach the world is through sometimes stubborn, oftentimes apathetic, and only occasionally motivated people who call themselves Christians, but who'd rather have material benefits than give of themselves to those whose body or spirit needs refreshing.

Us.

It's a choice He's made. A choice with benefits and consequences.

A benefit: Once He uses us, we realize there is nothing more fun or fulfilling we could ever do.

A consequence: **We don't always make ourselves available** to the individuals God wants to help through us, so their needs may not be met as God intended—and we miss out on the good thing He wanted us to be a part of.

21 } Abundant living comes in GIVING, not receiving.

While God is still doing incredible miracles throughout the earth, He wants us to be involved in the day-to-day joy of giving our lives away. Remember when Jesus said that he who finds his life must lose it, and he who loses his life will find it? What He was saying is that TRUE LIFE, REAL LIFE, ABUNDANT LIFE isn't found in meeting your own needs, but in meeting the needs of others! In other words, **a selfish pig can never be satisfied**—and will never be truly happy.

God wants to bless you by using you—and He will when you tell Him you're available. **When you're used for what you were created to be used for, you're happier, more fulfilled, and always more productive.**

Christians were made to give. Surviving and thriving as a follower of Christ is to take His example of not coming to be served, but to serve, and to give our lives for others.

Get INVOLVED in church.

Yeah. Yeah. Yeah. **We know you're busy.** But for those of you who think Sunday morning was created just for you to sleep in, THINK AGAIN! Or maybe you've got more creative excuses for skipping out on church:

• I had to bleach my jeans so I could get that faded look.

• It's my night to clean the kitchen. (How hard is it to throw McDonald's wrappers in the trash?)

• My cat is in labor.

• I *would* go to youth group tonight, but **I just have too much homework.** And if I don't do my homework, I'll be tempted to cheat. (No way. We're not falling for this one. And if you really *are* tempted to cheat, check out *Lockers, Lunch Lines, Chemistry, and Cliques,* one of our other books in this series.)

• None of my friends go to church. (Is it time to look for new friends?)

• I don't know anyone. (And the best way to get to know people is to stay home and watch *Home Improvement* reruns, right?)

• I don't have a ride. (You'd better live at least fifty miles away to *ever* use this one!)

• I don't want to. (**Finally, an honest response.** Hey, if you don't have any motivation to be there or to serve, there are likely bigger problems. Do us a MAJOR favor: Call your youth leader or Sunday school teacher tomorrow and tell him or her *why* you don't want to go.)

But don't be like some people who are only PLAYING church.

Sad, but true.

Whether it's teens or adults, some are showing up for all of the wrong reasons.

• They come to keep peace with a spouse (or Mom and Dad).

• They come because it's a habit.

• They come to be seen.

• They come to do business. (This is really sad because they're only there to make contacts with others in order to sell them something at a later date!)

• They come to meet guys (or girls).

They're all just playing church.

So what does God think about these people?

Naturally, He's sad they haven't found the true joy of being with Him. He'd much rather they were there to serve, encourage, learn, or worship. But the fact remains: He loves those who play church as much as those who go for the right reasons. And He'd probably rather have them in a place where they are more likely to learn something about Him than they will by sitting at home reading the Sunday paper, or catching Zs, or watching football.

If you haven't already noticed the "playing-church" people, you will. But don't be too hard on them—and don't let them affect how YOU view the church. Just realize they're a fact of life, learn from the experience, and **let God deal with them in His own good time.**

24. Be IMITATORS of God.

At least that's what Ephesians 5:1 tells us:

• From *The Living Bible*: **"Follow God's example in everything you do** just as a much loved child imitates his father."

• From the King James Version: "Be ye therefore followers of God, as dear children. . . ."

• From the Good News Bible: "Since you are God's dear children, you must try to be like him."

• From the New International Version: "Be imitators of God, therefore, as dearly loved children. . . ."

Doesn't really matter which version of the Bible you're reading. God's message is the same: Reflect Him. Echo His lifestyle. **Be an imitator.**

REALIZE God doesn't grade on a curve.

This is a REAL IMPORTANT one, so don't skip this page.

You know how teachers sometimes grade on a curve? They add up all the scores on a test, then take the top 10 percent and give them an A, the next 10 percent a B, etc. Then even if lots of kids mess up, they won't all flunk or get a bad grade.

The curve goes something like this:

Believe it or not, this is how some people think when it comes to heaven. They think that if they're as "good" as the top 50 or 60 percent of all the people in the world (they figure that's at least passing), that heaven is a sure thing when they die. (Some even think they can make it if they're in the top 90 percent! Only the real flunkies at the bottom—the murderers and stuff—are going to hell.) Their reasoning goes, *If I do more good things than bad things throughout my entire life—or don't mess up worse than most people—God won't dare keep me out of heaven.*

In other words, **they're gambling their entire eternal future** on the notion that God grades on a curve.

Bad bet.

There are tons of verses that make this line of thinking look incredibly stupid, but here are two of the main ones:

"Jesus answered, 'I am the way and the truth and the life. No one comes to the Father except through me'" (John 14:6, NIV).

"Salvation is found in no one else, for there is no other name under heaven given to men by which we must be saved" (Acts 4:12, NIV).

These verses show perfectly that **it's pass or fail.** You either go through Jesus to get to God, or you don't. No amount of good works, or money, or church services, or being "better" than others can gain God's eternal favor. **It's Jesus or nothing.**

And if you think about it long enough, this is the way it *should* be. This gives REALLY BAD people, who have done bad things their entire lives, a chance at heaven if they use Jesus Christ as their bridge to God. If this system wasn't in place, they would have no hope at all!

Be JESUS to your world.

No, we're not talking about walking on water or giving one of your neighbors 20/20 vision by putting mud on his eyes. **God's not asking you to do miracles;** He's simply asking you to reach out to those around you in His name.

• Darius McCrary (Eddie Winslow on ABC's *Family Matters*) spends every Thanksgiving serving dinner to the homeless in downtown L.A.

• Cari spends time making and serving soup in an Alabama soup kitchen.

• Mark and Julie make someone's day brighter by frequenting their local nursing home.

What could you do?

• Volunteer to wrap Christmas gifts for an elderly person.

• Offer to go grocery shopping for someone who's sick or just too busy to do it themselves.

• Tutor someone at school who's failing one of the subjects you're good at.

• **Volunteer** at your local library to be a reader for children's story time.

• Sit next to someone in the cafeteria who always sits by herself. (Talk to her, too.)

• If you hear that a classmate just lost someone close to him (a parent through death or divorce, a grandparent, a dog), drop him a note and just let him know you're sorry and that you'll pray for him.

• Be an encourager to someone who

needs some affirmation.

Being Jesus to those around you may not take much effort, but it *will* take time. The exciting part? The time spent investing some energy in someone else's life can make an eternal difference!

Heaven is a free gift, but FAITHFULNESS is what delivers in this life (though not always the way we expect).

Several of Jesus' parables conclude that **faithfulness in small things will give you the chance to be faithful in big things.** The rewards the parables name are leading more cities or owning larger plots of land. But if real estate and power aren't your goals, don't despair. Jesus was using these stories to illustrate a "Kingdom Principle." (A KP is a powerful and irrefutable truth.)

Many people have used this particular KP to make the point that if you're faithful with a small amount of money, **God will soon give you more with which to be faithful.** Faithfulness with money, as you may know, means giving away God's portion, but also spending the rest wisely. This application of the KP *can be* true, but it's not the only application. Nor does it always work that way. Remember the widow who gave her last two cents? This would have been a perfect chance for Jesus to make the point that if you give away all of your money, you'll get more. Well, she might have received more later, but we're not told. It's likely she was poor the rest of her life. And remember the time this rich guy came to Jesus saying he wanted eternal life and Jesus told him to go sell all he had, give the money to the poor, and then follow Him? Jesus could have sealed the deal with this guy by saying, "This will prove you can be trusted, and you'll get it all back with interest later." But He didn't.

We've both known **people who have been faithful** with a little money and were given much, much more later in life. And we've both known people who had a LOT of cash or possessions, but weren't even faithful with it all. (So why did they deserve to have all that money in the first place?)

Our point is that this KP isn't just talking about money. **What else can you be faithful with?** Are there other areas you want God to know you can be trusted in? We can think of tons of stuff!

You can . . .

• be faithful with one friend. (Perhaps God will trust you with more.)

• be faithful in your relationships with the opposite sex by staying pure.

(Perhaps God will give you a lifetime mate that far exceeds your expectations.)

• be faithful in your education. (Perhaps God will give you a scholarship when you least expect it.)

• be faithful and obedient to your parents. (Perhaps you'll have kids who are faithful and obedient to you when you become a parent.)

• be faithful on the job. (Perhaps God will allow you a better job.)

• be faithful in your time with God. (Perhaps He will show you parts of His character that you never knew before.)

The key word (obviously) is "faithfulness." But another key word is "perhaps." We can't **guarantee** what God will do as a reward to your faithfulness. We know He DOES reward faithfulness, but not always the way we *think* we want.

Faithfulness shouldn't be a way to manipulate

God into giving you things that are bigger and better. It should be the goal— period. If God sends extraordinary or unexpected blessing as a byproduct— great! If not, great!

Learn to ask yourself this question in everything you do: "How can I be faithful in what I'm doing today?"

The final and best reward for faithfulness is something Jesus himself will say to you when you meet Him face-to-face: " . . . Well done, good and faithful servant! . . . Come and share your master's happiness!" (Matthew 25:21, NIV).

SATURATE yourself with things of the Lord.

• **Memorize Scripture.** (Yes, this is the second time we've mentioned this!) Here's a good one to start with: "We are pressed on every side by troubles, but not crushed and broken. We are perplexed because we don't know why things happen as they do, but we don't give up and quit. We are hunted down, but God never abandons us. We get knocked down, but we get up again and keep going" (2 Corinthians 4:8–9, TLB).

• **Listen** to Christian music. Whatever your favorite sound is in secular music, you can find a similar sound in Christian music. The difference? The words.

• Get a Bible you're proud of and one that you understand. With all the student Bibles on the market today, there's NO EXCUSE for not having one you're crazy about.

• Find a good teen devotional book. No, not to replace the Bible. **God's Word is the ultimate devotional book.** We GOTTA read it every day to stay in tune with Him. But it's also fun to read a devotional book *alongside* your Bible reading. We suggest reading a short devotion in the morning and reading your Bible in the evening (or vice-versa).

• Don't miss church.

• **Rent** or purchase a Christian video. (There are some excellent *and* entertaining Christian videos out there. Find out for yourself.)

• Memorize your *Brio* or *Breakaway* magazine from cover to cover when it arrives in the mail each month. (Option #2: Read the cool articles.)

29 Be an ANDREW.

Andrew was the very first disciple chosen by Jesus, but he's never listed first in any mention of the twelve. Whenever the Gospels (Matthew, Mark, Luke, John) list the twelve disciples, he's always listed second—and even fourth in Mark and Acts. Who's listed first? Peter. *Always.*

We don't know very much about Andrew from what the Bible says, but we can imagine how he might have felt about this. If we were in Andrew's shoes we just might be a bit ticked for not being listed number one! But Andrew doesn't seem like the kind of guy to hold grudges. **He wasn't bitter.** He didn't mind playing second fiddle. You see, *he* knew that Peter could do things he couldn't. He was proud of his older brother. He didn't mind living in his shadow.

Andrew knew that Peter was STACKED with ability. He knew that through Peter God could do incredible things to impact the world. But he also knew that **God used everyday, ordinary guys** like himself—guys that had only one talent.

You see, Andrew had only one thing he could do well. Don't ever ask him to speak in front of a group. His knees would shake and his throat would go dry.

Never try to inspire him to take charge or be a leader—it just wasn't him.

But ask him to be friendly, and you've got a friend for life! The one thing that Andrew did well **was SMILE**. One-on-one, he was fantastic! He was known as the friendly apostle.

Besides being listed in the group of twelve disciples, Andrew's only mentioned three other times. And every single time, he's doing the same thing. He's bringing someone to Jesus. Wow! What a way to go down in history, huh?

He first brought himself, then his brother Peter. Next, he brought the boy with the fishes and loaves. Not long afterward, he brought some Gentile visitors from Greece. They had come a long distance to see Jesus. They approached Philip and asked if he would introduce them to the Messiah.

Philip didn't know what to do. He'd never seen Jesus minister to Gentiles before. What if His message of salvation was only for the Jews? *I know what I'll do,* he thought. *I'll take them to Andrew. Andrew is friends with everyone! He'll know what to do.*

And what did Andrew do? He took them straight to Jesus. And the Master's own heart was stirred. He looked at Andrew and the Gentiles and said, "They will come from the east and the west, from the north and the south, and sit down in the kingdom of God" (Luke 13:29, NKJV).

If Andrew hadn't introduced the visitors from Greece to Jesus, we may not have known that **salvation is for <u>everyone</u>, not only a select few.**

You don't have to be a leader, the life of the party, or the most talented to be used by God. Everyone can't be a Peter. Everyone *can*, however, be an Andrew.

Who can YOU bring to Jesus? Stop reading RIGHT NOW and ask God to bring to your mind the names of three people who aren't Christians. Commit to pray for these people every day. Ask God what *specific* things you can do to help them see Jesus in you.

Heaven is real—GUARANTEED—and so is hell.

Guarantees in this life don't always seem too positive. Jesus guarantees trial and tribulation, but He also says He'll walk through it with us. He guarantees our faith will be tested—but that's just to purify it. The Bible talks about hell and eternity a lot, but it also mentions heaven about the same amount.

We've both learned through the years that **if the Bible talks about it, it's TOTALLY TRUE.** There are others in the world who decide it's OK to pick and choose what part of the Bible is true. The best example is the death and resurrection of Jesus Christ. Most believe Jesus walked this earth, and most can agree that Jesus probably died by crucifixion, but many just can't buy into the fact that He rose from the dead and is still alive today. If people were to believe that, it would have serious implications about how they live their lives. After all, if Jesus is still alive, that means EVERYTHING He said is true—and He really IS God.

The bottom line is that **Jesus IS still alive, and everything He said IS true**—including the parts about heaven and hell. It is impossible to say you have Jesus in your heart and life without accepting His Word as truth.

God wants to be the HUB of the wheel, not a spoke.

When I (Greg) first became a Christian my freshman year in college, a lot of things were important in my life: school, my girlfriend, a few closer friends, sports . . . and *Star Trek* reruns. God seemed to round out the puzzle. With salvation, I had it all. And that's the way it stayed for about a year. I kept all of my priorities, occasionally read my Bible, and, even less often, went to church.

Everything in my life was a spoke, including God. Though I knew I had something different, I didn't recognize Him as the strongest part of my life.

The strongest part of a bike is the steel-alloy hub of the bike tire. It's made strong because everything else connected to it is dependent on the hub's strength. A weak hub means the spokes will collapse.

That first year my Christian faith was weak. It was then someone pointed out that the likely reason was because God was just an add-on, not the center.

Ever feel like a sickly, weak Christian? Maybe God is a spoke instead of the hub.

Just as accepting salvation is a decision of the will—a choice—made because God was prompting your heart to trust Him, so the Christian life is a series of choices. Lordship choices.

Who is going to be in the center? You? Your boyfriend? Sports? Friends? . . . Or God?

If you're ready to choose God,

God's ready to be chosen. He doesn't force himself

into the hub position; He waits for an invitation.

The invitation is your first step. Obedience is the second. God desires that we KEEP Him as the hub of our lives every single day by choosing Him as Lord. But He doesn't force us to obey; He waits patiently for us to choose.

You'll be faced with lordship choices every day. No, you won't always make the right choices. Perhaps you won't even bat .200. But **God DOES see the heart.** When your heart wants to obey, you'll know that God is the strongest part of your life—the HUB, not just a spoke.

Ever heard the saying, "You may be the only BIBLE that people around you are reading?"

Well, it's true.

Know what that means?

Means **you'd better be worth reading.**

Enough said.

33 Be a PETER.

Well, *somebody* had to be the leader of the twelve disciples. *Someone* had to be president. And it seemed as if **Peter was always that way.** Even as a child, he probably ran the fastest, swam the deepest, climbed the highest, and stood in the spotlight on every fishing expedition.

And now, in the Bible, he's *still* in the spotlight. He's usually the first to speak and the first to act. He's spontaneous. Many times he blurts something out without having thought it through first. Remember the time he brags he'll never betray Jesus? Only a few hours later he's already denied that he even knows Him—not once but **THREE** times!

He's impulsive. (Remember that walking-on-water incident?) And he's influential. (Check out the book of Acts for the scoop on Peter preaching to 3,000 people and leading them *all* to the Lord!)

Maybe his brother, Andrew, was an ordinary guy. And maybe many of the other disciples were everyday men. But Peter? He was no average guy. For every talent anyone else had, he had more.

It seemed like he could do it all! **He was probably the quarterback of Bethsaida High School's football team** ... the lead in every play ... the star ... always in the spotlight. He never had to worry about girls—they called *him*!

Even Jesus said to Peter, "You're the ROCK. You're just the kind of person I can build My church upon." Wow. Wouldn't THAT feel good? What a compliment! What an honor.

But the path to *becoming* a rock—the path to becoming solid, consistent, and stable in his relationship with Christ—was no easy path.

One minute the Rock—the next minute the voice of Satan! Jesus was talking about the future and all that would happen to Him. When He mentioned the crucifixion and the persecution that would follow, Peter impulsively blurted out, "No, Lord! We'll NEVER let that happen!" Jesus told him that he had the voice of the devil for trying to interfere with God's plans.

It wasn't until the night of Jesus' trials that Peter finally realized he couldn't be a ROCK in his own strength. He was too weak. He'd just denied Christ three times. How could he ever be strong enough to lay the foundation for the future church if he couldn't even stand up to the pressure of a servant girl?

That night, in his *weakness*, Peter learned an important lesson: **It's through our weakness that God's strength shines.**

You see, *none* of us can *ever* be strong enough, cool enough, or talented enough to be all that God calls us to be. It's only when we DIE to ourselves and give up our will for HIS will that He pours His spirit of strength and power into us.

That night, Peter died. No, not physically. He died to his self-centeredness and to the desire to run things *his* way. He died to his impulsive and self-reliant nature. And he came ALIVE to God's strength, God's plans, God's will, God's way. In other words, Peter *yielded*.

Hmmm. WE need to learn that lesson, too, don't we? **Not all of us can be a multitalented Peter.** But all of us CAN be rock-solid in our relationship with Christ as Peter eventually was.

But not until we're totally submissive. Not until we "give up" and put God on the throne of our lives can we ever reach that point of rock-solidness.

The world is full of weak-kneed, wishy-washy, surface-level Christians. What

God needs and wants are DISCIPLES who are committed to His Lordship. Only then can God change the world through us.

Are you ROCK-SOLID in your walk with Christ? You *can* be! If not, WHY not?

34. Not EVERYONE thinks Jesus Christ is God's Son.

If they don't think Jesus was God's Son, who do they think He was?

• A good teacher.

• A born liar.

• A crazy man.

• A vague historical figure blown out of proportion by a group of fanatical followers.

• A myth.

What many people really want is to keep Jesus as someone they can control by devaluing Him. Very logical. After all, if you can devalue God, you can put yourself in His place. You can stay in control of your life every step of the way, and not answer to anyone. The only moral choices are the ones you make. There's no such thing as immoral behavior because there is no standard besides government laws.

How will someone act around you—someone who believes Jesus ISN'T God's Son? Every way imaginable. As you get older, unbelievers have a tendency to dig in their heels and get more antagonistic. Since they have stayed in control of their lives for so long, they're used to it. They don't want ANYONE hinting to them there's another way. But since you're younger, you'll find that many of your friends aren't as close-minded. As a teenager, you're at the best time in your life for sharing your faith. Friends aren't as likely to get mad at you for letting them know **someone else is in control of your life, and they should consider letting Him be**

in control of theirs. (For more information on how to share your faith, check out the book we mentioned earlier, *Keeping Your Cool While Sharing Your Faith*). It's not about not getting mad; it's about having Jesus in your life and having conversations in a natural way.)

35} INVITE your friends to church.

Especially the ones who are considering Jesus.

Someone you've never talked to about the Lord may not understand all that's happening. It may even scare them away. But for others, it's the natural next step to learning more of who God is and what Jesus did for them.

36. Be a STAR.

Dare to act differently than non-Christians do. **Risk being kind to a loner or a geek.** Be nice to your teachers. Show respect for authority. Obey your parents. Why? So you can be a STAR that shines so brightly others can't *help* but notice.

"Do everything without complaining or arguing, so that you may become blameless and pure, children of God without fault in a crooked and depraved generation, in which you **SHINE LIKE STARS** in the universe. . . ." (Philippians 2:14–15, NIV, authors' emphasis).

37 EXPECT conflict.

If you're going to be a committed disciple, realize that **you're going to have head-on conflict with the world's system.** And that's no surprise, really. Jesus warned us it would be like that. The issue isn't that you face tough times. (Thank God for those times, because they prove He's true to His Word.) The issue is: Are you going to be more concerned with what the world thinks or with what your heavenly Father thinks?

Here's some ammunition (from *The Living Bible*) to jot down on 3 x 5 cards and stick inside your notebook or your locker:

"Happy are those who are persecuted because they are good, for the Kingdom of Heaven is theirs" (Matthew 5:10).

"The people of God who are destined for prison will be arrested and taken away; those destined for death will be killed. But do not be dismayed, for here is your opportunity for endurance and confidence" (Revelation 13:10).

"It is quite true that the way to live a godly life is not an easy matter. But the answer lies in Christ. . . ." (1 Timothy 3:16).

" . . . in the last days it is going to be very difficult to be a Christian" (2 Timothy 3:1).

"If you want to **keep from becoming fainthearted and weary,** think about his patience as sinful men did such terrible things to him. After all, you have never yet struggled against sin and temptation until you sweat great drops of blood" (Hebrews 12:4).

"So take a new grip with your tired hands, stand firm on your shaky legs, and mark out a straight, smooth path for your feet so that those who follow you, though weak and lame, will not fall and hurt themselves, but become strong" (Hebrews 12:12–13).

"I will never, *never* fail you nor forsake you" (Hebrews 13:5).

". . . is your life full of difficulties and temptations? Then be happy, for when the way is rough, your patience has a chance to grow. So let it grow, and don't try to squirm out of your problems. For when your patience is finally in full bloom, then you will be ready for anything, strong in character, full and complete" (James 1:2–4).

So be truly glad! There is wonderful joy ahead, even though the going is rough for a while down here.

"These trials are only to test your faith, to see whether or not it is strong and pure. It is being tested as fire tests gold and purifies it—and your faith is far more precious to God than mere gold; so if your faith remains strong after being tried in the test tube of fiery trials, it will bring you much praise and glory and honor on the day of his return" (1 Peter 1:6–7).

"Be careful—watch out for attacks from Satan, your great enemy. He prowls around like a hungry, roaring lion, looking for some victim to tear apart. Stand firm when he attacks. Trust the Lord; and remember that other Christians all around the world are going through these sufferings too" (1 Peter 5:8–9).

"After you have suffered a little while, our God, who is full of kindness through Christ, will give you his eternal glory. He **PERSONALLY** will come and pick you up, and set you firmly in place, and make you stronger than ever" (1 Peter 5:10, authors' emphasis).

SUPPORT your youth leaders.

Want to know who's the most underpaid—and usually under-appreciated—person in leadership at your church?

Most of the time, you don't have to look any farther than the youth leader. If you're in a small church with volunteer youth leaders . . . well, let's just say their reward is coming later—in heaven.

It's tough work spending time with teenagers if you're an adult. Not only do older people wonder why you don't get a "real job," but some teens wonder why you'd want to hang around younger kids. They might think you're weird.

Such is the dilemma faced by youth leaders. Though God has told them to give their lives away to younger people, others misunderstand their intentions.

You can make your youth leaders' day . . . week . . . month . . . maybe even year by showing a little genuine appreciation for all of their efforts. Whether you have one or twelve leaders, there are little things you can do to let them know their work isn't going unnoticed:

• A genuine handshake (make eye contact) and tell them, "Thanks for all you're doing with this group—and with me."

• A card or letter always makes a **great statement.** We both have kept a file full of letters from our youth leader days from those who took the time and effort to send them. They're more precious to us than gold.

• Organize your group to throw a party for the youth workers who have donated so many hours to you.

• Ask the pastor if you and a few others can go up front at church and let everyone in the congregation know the kind of adults they have giving their lives away to the youth. But don't let the youth leaders know you're going to do it. You'll probably see them speechless for the first time! (They might even cry!)

• Collect some money and buy them gifts for holidays and birthdays, or whatever.

• Get a picture taken of your group and blow it up to at least 8 x 10. Then put it in a frame with some nice words and everyone's signature.

• Have some rich person in the church donate money to send them to the Bahamas! (This will insure they'll NEVER leave your church!)

Show your appreciation to them whenever you can. You'll feel good; they'll feel good. Hey, it's the right thing!

If you don't have youth leaders, DARE to become one!

Since most churches are small, it's sometimes tough to convince a busy adult or college student to be in charge of youth activities or to arrange teen Bible studies.

Have you ever thought about this before? If no one steps up to lead, why don't YOU lead! Either form a committee of friends or just do it yourself. Get a parent or adult to serve as an adviser if you can, then take the bull by the horns. And don't worry about whether a ton of other kids in the church will follow. *Something* is always better than *nothing*.

No, you probably won't have people thanking you for your efforts, but God WILL reward you. Don't worry about taking the credit either. In fact, the group will be more successful if you can deflect the credit to other people who help. The reason? Motives aren't always trusted. Some may feel you're just trying to be in control. If you can get something off the ground . . . a breakfast Bible study, a video night followed by a prayer time, a Sunday singspiration where you try to gather every teenager within twenty miles for an hour of a capella hymn singing by memory . . . well, maybe not.

Be creative.

Enlist other friends to help. (Those you like, and those you don't know very well.)

Get an adult to advise you so you don't do something dumb or sacrilegious (like a Nine Inch Nails look-alike contest, toga party, or a kegger.)

Lead out! You can do it!

40 BE a Barnabas or a Dorcas.

Barnabas was known for encouraging people. In fact, his name means "one who encourages." He was a great asset to Paul. Remember when he was still called Saul and he hit the "blind spot" on the road to Damascus? Now, this was no ordinary sunlight. This light was so bright, not even Raybans could've protected him from it! It was so strong, it knocked him down and blinded him!

After God changed Saul's name to Paul, **gave him back his 20/20,** and healed him spiritually, he was ready to spread the Good News. The only problem was, the Christians were scared to death of him!

After all, he *had* been on a rampage! He was known for wiping OUT the believers. Now he was claiming to BE one of them.

Hmmm. You'd probably think twice, too, before opening *your* door to the guy. But not Barnabas. Good ol' Barney not only welcomed him with open arms, but he also *encouraged* him in his new-found faith.

Where would we be today if it hadn't been for Barnabas's willingness to accept someone whom everyone else doubted? Kinda makes you think, doesn't it? **Is there someone YOU should be accepting and encouraging?**

And then there's Dorcas. Here's a woman who had a wonderful impact on her whole community! The Bible tells us that she was always doing good, kind things for others. When she died, the whole town mourned. When Peter heard about her death, he walked into her room, knelt, and prayed. THEN he commanded her to get up! And she *did*! The town was never the same. (Read the whole story in Acts 9.)

Would you like to change your reputation?
Then resolve to be a Dorcas (constantly look for ways you can help others) or a Barnabas (strive to encourage those around you).

Know what would happen if YOU became a Dorcas or a Barnabas? *Your* town would never be the same, either!

41. Does God answer ALL of our prayers?

Yes, He does . . . in four ways:

1. "Yes." This is by far the favorite way to have our prayers answered. Yet if EVERY prayer was answered *yes*, we'd most likely be miserable.

2. "No." Not quite as popular as *yes*, yet *no* has some distinct advantages. *No* keeps us from getting things that are actually selfish requests. It protects us from an unhappy future and, generally, allows God to be God and us to be the obedient followers. When He *does* say *no*, it's not simply to remind us who's boss. God says *no* out of genuine concern for the big picture of our lives.

It's tougher, but you ought to thank Him as much for the nos as for the yeses.

3. "Wait" or "Maybe." Both imply the dreaded "Not until Christmas" response we used to hear our parents say. Remember when you wanted a new coat or toy or bike in October, and the standard response was, "Christmas is just around the corner"? Sometimes we got what we wanted; sometimes we didn't.

Again, this response isn't as popular as a quick *yes*, but it's often the best. What if you prayed for a job so you could afford the insurance on a 1976 Gremlin or a 1977 Pacer (or some other wonderful classic car you'd never think about driving—let alone owning—in a million years). Yet while you were praying for a job . . . every night . . . on your knees . . . with two or more people gathered together . . . in faith and confidence as you approached the throne of grace—

God's plan was slightly different. His goals were:

• Protecting you from getting into an accident on a snowy night in January or a drunk driver on New Year's Eve.

• Keeping you away from temptation because He knows there's this girl with lesser morals who would pursue you and who has been known to spend too much time steaming up windows in every car imaginable.

• He doesn't want you to work during high school because you need to practice your "set" and "spikes" because He wants to give you a volleyball scholarship to UCLA so you can make it to the Olympics in 2004 and win a gold medal and tell the world how much your family and God mean to you, and put you on TV endorsing Nike products and on the cover of Wheaties boxes so that whenever someone sees you they think of how much they want to be just like you! (*Hey, it could happen.*)

So if you knew the big picture, what would you really want?

A job today flipping burgers at $4.23 an hour so you could drive a car you really don't want to drive anyway, or a bazillion dollars in endorsement money ten years from now (though money isn't your motivation in life) and the chance to point to Jesus Christ as the center of your life in front of millions of people?

Our picture of what is a good short-term and/or long-term future isn't always God's. **Be patient.** Accept the *waits* and *maybes* you get from God. **Don't grumble.** Thank Him for them, and take what comes. It's usually better than what you wanted in the first place.

4. "I told you that already!" A lot of times we pray for things that God has already said are pretty lame. (Did He really say they were "lame"? Well . . . maybe

that wasn't the exact word He used, but when He helps us interpret the Bible today, He helps us realize these things *are* lame.) For instance:

• "God, make me popular." (We're actually asking for the approval of people, rather than God.)

• "Lord, **I want to be rich** so I can give lots of money away." (Remember, it's easier for a rich man to go through the eye of a needle than to enter the Kingdom of Heaven.)

• "Father, change my appearance so I can like myself better." (Read Psalm 139. You're pretty special already!)

Some of our prayers have already been answered. The answers are in black-and-white in that book by our beds. **So read what the book tells you to do … and do it!** (For more thoughts on this subject, grab a book Susie wrote called *Stuff You Don't Have to Pray About* [Broadman & Holman Publishers]. It'll *really* put things in perspective!)

Whenever you pray—for whatever reason—you need to start trusting God to actually answer your prayer in the way HE wants, not the way you think would be best. A good habit to get into is repeating the heartfelt words God loves to hear: "Your will be done."

God has a terrific sense of humor. Learn to LAUGH with Him.

42

What makes God laugh?

• The dumb things we say when we think what we're saying is so wise.

• The quirky little things we do.

• The way we get so worked up about things that really are in His control anyway.

• What we try to get away with when others aren't looking. Actually, He's probably not laughing at this one since **He sees everything.** But it's funny when we think we've done something in total secrecy, and the fact is: God and the angels are looking on. (This is probably more embarrassing than funny. But God understands that imperfect humans will do dumb stuff. Ever wonder if God and the angels point at us and say, "Look, Matt's trying to get away with another 'stupid human trick'"?)

Be serious about the serious stuff, but don't sweat most of it. If you can laugh—or at least smile—at life and all of its twists and turns, you'll be happier.

43 God's plan for your life WILL be fulfilled.

Memorize this for those times when doubts take over:

"But these things I plan won't happen right away. Slowly, steadily, surely, the time approaches when the vision will be fulfilled. If it seems slow, do not despair, for these things will surely come to pass. Just be patient! They will not be overdue a single day!" (Habakkuk 2:3, TLB).

In other words, **God is never early . . . but He's also never late.**

44 Know how to LEAD someone to Christ.

Not many have the chance to be there when someone else comes into the Kingdom of God, but if you happen to be in that position, here are a few things to remember.

First of all, it's God's job to save people, not yours. It's very cool to be the one to pray with people as they trust Christ for the first time, but don't feel as though you haven't done anything to help them along if you're not the one to lead them in prayer. A lot of the hard work happens before people accept Christ anyway. **They have to see you and other Christians in action.** They have an information gap about the truth of what Jesus did for them that has to be filled, and the Holy Spirit has to draw them to repentance. That's why at big crusades so many people come forward. Most likely, Christians have been praying and sharing with them for months (perhaps years). They were ready.

Second, you can't actually *fail* at leading someone to Christ. More than likely you're doing your best in explaining things as you know them. Remember, God has to be dealing with them, and they have to choose.

Third, you can *sort of* fail if you miss some key points. **Making the choice to trust Christ is a big decision.** If you've been sharing with a friend, you want to make sure they have all of the information. The reason? When they DO make a decision, they will have made an informed one. They knew the benefits *and* the costs.

So how do you lead someone down that road to a relationship with Jesus

Christ? There are several methods. One of the better ones that is easy to remember is called the "Roman Road of Salvation." It takes four passages from the book of Romans to tell the story. Here's how it goes:

1. *Romans 3:23:* " . . . for all have sinned and fall short of the glory of God . . . " (NIV).

Unless your friends recognize there is a brick wall between them and God—a wall caused by a disobedient and sinful nature they can't get rid of on their own—they won't see a need to have the Savior.

QUESTIONS:

• Do you recognize that there's nothing you can do to measure up to God's standard?

• Do you know that no amount of good works, money, or church attendance can take away your sin? (If they answer yes, move on to . . .)

TRANSITION:

• This was a real dilemma for God, but He did something totally unexpected. Instead of deserting His creation or destroying us, He decided to make a way possible for us to know Him again. He loved us enough to make a way for us to find Him.

2. *Romans 5:6:* "You see, at the right time, when we were still powerless, Christ died for the ungodly" (NIV).

QUESTIONS:

• Do you know about this fact?

• What more can I tell you about Jesus Christ that you don't know?

TRANSITION:

Though God came back to find us, there is still something that had to be done about our sin, our natural tendency to shake our fist at God and run our own lives.

3. *Romans 6:23:* "For the wages of sin is death, but the gift of God is eternal life in Christ Jesus our Lord" (NIV).

QUESTIONS:

• Do you understand why Jesus' death on the cross was God's gift to us? (If not, then explain how God put everyone's sin on Jesus, then killed it.)

• Do you want to reach out and take this free gift?

TRANSITION:

• A gift can't be used unless it is received. The way to receive God's free gift is by telling Him you want it—not just with your mouth, but with your heart, as well.

4. *Romans 10:9–10:* " . . . if you confess with your mouth, 'Jesus is Lord,' and believe in your heart that God raised him from the dead, you will be saved. For it is with your heart that you believe and are justified, and it is with your mouth that you confess and are saved" (NIV).

QUESTIONS:

• What's holding you back from asking Jesus Christ to forgive your sin and come into your life?

• Would you like to pray right now?

TRANSITION:

If so, you can repeat this prayer after me:

"Lord Jesus, I admit to you something you already know: I'm a sinner. I realize there is nothing I can do on my own to get rid of my sin. I know it's the one thing that separates you and me, and I don't want that separation any longer. Forgive my sin and take it away. Come into my life and make me a new person. Help me to follow you and learn more about you. I want to give my life to you. Amen."

Tell your friends at this point that **all of the angels in heaven rejoice when a soul turns to God!**

For your friends, the even harder part begins now: *growing* as a Christian. Your friends are going to need to have a Bible they can understand and know where to start reading. Talk with them soon about getting involved in a church. And they need you and other Christians praying for them constantly because **the devil is going to be really ticked off.**

There's obviously more that could be mentioned (and it IS important to be thorough), but space doesn't allow us to talk about the whole area of sharing your faith. Earlier, we mentioned a book you'll find helpful: *Keeping Your Cool While Sharing Your Faith.* Check it out.

Keep your eyes on JESUS CHRIST—not on people, things, or abilities.

Only ONE Person holds the right key.

The key opens the door.

The right key opens the right doors.

You want to go through the RIGHT doors. (Right?)

Follow the One with the right key.

He opens the right doors.

When we take our eyes off of the KeyMaster and put it on people or things *we think* hold the key, such as . . .

- our parents
- our friends
- our abilities
- our looks
- our teachers or leaders
- our money

. . . then we walk through the wrong doors. We make BIG mistakes.

Things can never give us the key to the right door. And people cannot give us the key to the right door either, but they CAN help us find the door by *pointing* to the KeyMaster as the One who holds the answers.

To *see* correctly, your eyes must be focused so you don't stumble.

To *walk* correctly, they must be focused in the right direction.

Jesus Christ is the right direction.

Living God's way depends on going the right direction.

Church will sometimes get BORING.

But here's what to do . . .

- Take notes.

- Pray to stay focused.

- Have a mint.

- Take five deep breaths.

Read some great Bible chapters so God has a chance to speak to you: Romans 8; Romans 12; John 14, 15, 16; Ephesians 5 and 6; Hebrews 11; 1 John 5; Psalms 51, 104, or 139; Proverbs 16; Matthew 24 and 25; 1 Corinthians 13.

47. Keep GROWING spiritually.

In 2 Peter, God gives us a fantastic recipe for spiritual growth. (OK, guys, *you* can scratch out the *recipe* word and replace it with *strategy*. Sound better?)

"Do you want more and more of God's kindness and peace? Then learn to know him better and better. For as you know him better, he will give you, through his great power, everything you need for living a truly good life: he even shares his own glory and his own goodness with us! And by that same mighty power he has given us all the other rich and wonderful blessings he promised; for instance, the promise to save us from the lust and rottenness all around us, and to give us his own character. But **to obtain these gifts, you need more than faith;** you must also work hard to be good, and even that is not enough. For then you must learn to know God better and discover what he wants you to do. Next, learn to put aside your own desires so that you will become patient and godly, gladly letting God have his way with you. This will make possible the next step, which is for you to enjoy other people and to like them, and finally you will grow to love them deeply. The more you go on in this way, the more you will grow strong spiritually and become fruitful and useful to our Lord Jesus Christ" (2 Peter 1:2–8, TLB).

So what's first?

1. Lay the foundation. Ask Christ to invade your life with His love and for-

giveness.

2. Get to KNOW Him better and better. How? **Read His Word and talk to Him on a daily basis.** (Sound familiar? We keep repeating it because it's so essential!)

3. Ask for His power to permeate the very core of your being.

4. In His power, and in His strength, determine to live ABOVE the rotten things of the world (lust, pride, selfishness, arguing, cheating, cursing, wrong thoughts).

5. Exercise your faith.

6. Do good to those around you.

7. Seek God's will on a daily basis. (This means not simply asking about His will for your career or college plans or future spouse, but seeking His will every single day—in the ordinary things as well as the big stuff.)

8. Don't settle for just making Him #1 in your life. **Make Him your life!** Allow Him to reshape and mold you in His image.

9. Love those around you. Learn to enjoy the company of other believers—even if they're different from you. Relax in the fact that you share a common bond—Jesus Christ. Be excited that you'll spend eternity together with your brothers and sisters in the Lord. Celebrate being a part of His family!

10. Exercise the fruit of the spirit. (For a listing of the main menu, check out Galatians 5:22–23.)

Read CHRISTIAN material.

Why? Because it will help you establish a godly frame of mind. You see, *mind-set is important.* **Whatever we think about is eventually what we'll act upon.** (For more info on this, flip over to section 16: "Garbage in = Garbage Out.")

Here are our suggestions:

• Become a member of *Brio* (for teen girls) or *Breakaway* (for teen guys), Focus on the Family's monthly magazines for youth. The price? Only about as much as a large pizza—heavy on the toppings. Want a free sample? Call 1-800-232-6459.

• Like romance and intrigue? (OK, guys, you can go lift weights for a sec while we chat with the girls.) Then consider shoving your nose into some of *these* series from Bethany House Publishers: WHITE DOVE ROMANCES, LIVE! FROM BRENTWOOD HIGH, SPRINGSONG BOOKS, JENNIE MCGRADY MYSTERIES, and CEDAR RIVER DAYDREAMS.

• **Concerned about the opposite sex?** Grab hold of *What Hollywood Won't Tell You About Sex, Love and Dating* by Greg Johnson and Susie Shellenberger (Regal Publishing).

• Like THIS book? Then get the other three in this series: *Lockers, Lunch Lines, Chemistry, and Cliques; Cars, Curfews, Parties, and Parents; Life, Love, Music, and Money* (Bethany House Publishers).

• Have a friend whose parents have split? You can help by giving them a copy of *Keeping Your Life Together When Your Parents Pull Apart* by Angela Elwell Hunt (Tyndale House Publishers).

• **Want to know more about** Christians who are into college and pro sports? Then check out *Sports Spectrum* magazine at your local Christian bookstore. (Call first to make sure they have it.)

How to KNOW "fer shure" that you're going to heaven.

"And this is the testimony: God has given us eternal life, and this life is in his Son. He who has the Son has life; he who does not have the Son of God does not have life.

"I write these things to you who believe in the name of the Son of God so that you may know that you have eternal life" (1 John 5:11–13, NIV).

If you have the Son (Jesus), you have eternal life.

If you don't *feel* that you have the Son, point to this passage and tell the liar who's feeding you falsehoods (Satan) that you *do* have the Son. So back off!

Remember, the Bible doesn't say we have to be perfect to go to heaven (that was Jesus' job).

It doesn't say that if we have fleeting doubts, we're not saved.

It doesn't say we have to understand everything in the Bible.

It doesn't say we have to have all of the answers.

Repent.

Believe.

Know.

And live it!

That's eternal life!

50. SING in church.

Even if you can't sing on key, sing. It'll be good practice for when you get to heaven.

Even if you're a guy and hate to sing, sing anyway. Your voice will change soon, and you may be the next Michael W. Smith!

Even if someone says you sing like a sick cow, say "Thanks," and keep on singing, hoping you'll move up to sick moose or sick antelope in the near future.

It'll impress your parents. (But don't sing to try to impress them; just know it WILL impress them.)

It'll please God. And He doesn't care a bit how you sound. In fact, He knows exactly how you sound and wants to hear you sing anyway. If you've read through the Psalms, you know how often it talks about singing praises to God. But not once does it mention that you have to sing on key!

51. Make reading the Bible a good HABIT.

You know how you don't always LIKE to brush your teeth? But you always do? Because it's just the right thing to do (and because if you don't, your teeth will eventually fall out, and then when you try to say, "Hi, my name's Scott," it'll come out sounding like, "I, yi yay's Yodd," and **people will look at you funny because you sound like a foreigner** but look like a local and when all your friends are eating corn on the cob, you'll take a piece too, because you want to be included and be like everyone else, only you won't be able to get any of the corn off because you have no teeth, but you'll try anyway because **you don't want anyone to find out you're different** and you'll try to lip it off or scrape a few kernels with your gums but it just won't work and eventually the people sitting around you WILL notice and they'll put their own corn down to stare at you and thirty minutes later when your gums are bleeding and you've still got a full ear of corn on your cob, you'll realize that your friends are all laughing and pointing and saying, "Hey, what's with Yodd? **He's our age but he has no teeth** and it's totally gross," and finally they'll all get up to leave because their corn is cold and they don't want it anymore, and you'll be left alone with bleeding gums and butter smeared all over your face with some salt and pepper dabbed on for good measure and you'll WISH you had just brushed your teeth when your parents TOLD you to instead of only wetting the toothbrush and squeezing some toothpaste into the trash can to fool them. See, you can fool them *part* of the time, but eventually it's YOU who'll end up with no teeth and no friends and greasy Parkay on your skin [which has enough natural grease, anyway!] and you'll be all alone writing run-on sentences.)

Well, reading the Bible is kind of like that. **You just need to develop it as a good habit,** because if you don't, you'll eventually end up a mess.

" . . . See that you go on growing in the Lord . . ." (Colossians 2:7, TLB).

Don't be a spiritual ASSASSIN.

"Thou shalt not kill" means a lot more than just stabbing someone twenty-eight times. Did you know you can kill someone spiritually? What if your best friend, Jeremy, had a terrible Saturday night? He's angry with his parents, and his girlfriend just dumped him. He really *needs* to hear what Pastor Evans is saying on Sunday morning, but you keep sending him notes and trying to get his attention. You could actually be committing spiritual murder. Pretty scary, huh?

Learn to listen. And encourage those around you to listen, too.

Make a "True Love Waits" COMMITMENT.

You already know what the Bible says about premarital sex. (If you forgot, here's a basic refresher: IT'S WRONG!) But **have you made an actual pledge to remain sexually pure until marriage?**

Thousands (probably even millions) of teens are making this vow, and some of them are even *wearing* outward signs of their commitment—such as a necklace or keychain that serves as a chastity symbol. Maybe you already have one that you keep with you as a constant reminder of your commitment to purity.

If you *don't* have a chastity symbol, and if you want to wear your pledge, consider investing in a "True Love Waits" ring. It's a really cool 14K gold ring that has "True Love Waits" engraved on the outside.

These rings are available in three different widths, and you can get all the information by calling Factory 79 (the place that makes and sells them) at 1-800-677-0832. Tell them you want information on the ring that Susie wears. That's right—I'm still single, and I'm wearing my commitment.

You can also use it as a conversation-starter among your non-Christian friends. If you haven't made a "True Love Waits" pledge—and want to—you can do it right now. Here it is:

Believing that TRUE LOVE WAITS, I make a commitment to God, myself, my family, my friends, my future mate, and my future children to be sexually abstinent from this day until the day I enter a biblical marriage relationship.

Consider having a "True Love Waits" emphasis with your youth group. You can get all kinds of great material to pull it off (T-shirts, cassette tapes, brochures, etc.) by calling the **"True Love Waits" information line at 1-800-588-9248.**

Chewing gum during church WON'T send you to hell...

. . . but it sure can be rude. **You want to give God your very best, don't you?** That means your manners, the way you dress, how you act. This is *His* house. **Learn to be respectful.**

55} It's OK to be narrow-minded.

After all, you're walking a narrow road. (See Matthew 7:14.) So when others are ragging on you to "adjust" your morality, *don't compromise.*

And don't even THINK of using the phrase, "But everyone else . . ." That doesn't even hold water. Not *everyone* is living a holy life. **God calls you to a higher level and a deeper commitment.** And that means walking a narrow road—not a "holier-than-thou" road, a narrow road. (There's a difference. Your goal is to be humble, not proud.)

So go ahead. **Be narrow-minded.** In the best possible way.

Don't make SENSE.

God's logic doesn't always match up with *our* logic. To the world, God's logic is nonsense. Even so, it's still smarter than the wisest thing *we* could ever come up with. So don't make sense to the world; **accept God's logic.**

God's Logic: The least shall be the greatest.

The first shall be last.

The poor will become rich.

To live we must die.

The world's logic: God is love.

Love is blind.

Therefore, God is blind.

Or . . .

Stevie Wonder is God?

See, even our best attempts to make sense aren't as good as God's sometimes incomprehensible logic. And when you put your faith in God's logic—even though you may not understand it—**it will eventually prove to be the wisest decision you've ever made.** So wise, in fact, that it'll last through eternity.

Now, THAT makes sense!

Praying doesn't ALWAYS mean asking for help.

Remember when we said that God answers prayer in four ways? We hope you got the point that **God answers ALL of your prayers.** The key isn't tossing Him easy stuff all the time or only going to Him with the tough stuff. The key is taking *everything* to Him *all the time.* He loves it when we're in constant contact with Him throughout the day. It shows Him how much we value the RELATIONSHIP.

Ask Him for whatever you think you should, but don't just talk to Him when you want something. (Imagine how your parents would feel if the only time you talked to THEM was when you wanted something.)

58} DON'T be afraid!

Jesus' first words out of the tomb on Easter morning were, "Don't be afraid." He didn't come to scare us, but to love us.

There are 365 "fear nots" mentioned in the Bible. Do you think God is trying to tell us something?

If you're afraid of God, you don't understand His character. Here's a real clear

snapshot of what God is like: "For I know the plans I have for you, says the Lord. They are plans for good and not for evil, to give you a future and a hope" (Jeremiah 29:11, TLB).

And *your* role? **Let God love you** . . . reeeeeally love you. When you learn to bask in His love, the fear dissolves. "We need have no fear of someone who loves us perfectly; his perfect love for us eliminates all dread of what he might do to us. If we are afraid, it is for fear of what he might do to us, and shows that we are not fully convinced that he really loves us" (1 John 4:18, TLB).

Still scared? Don't be. Save your fear for something worth screaming over . . . like the dirty clothes underneath your bed. Now THAT'S scary!

Be a summer MISSIONARY.

Lots of teens do it! Consider giving up one of your summers to make a difference in the lives of others. Here are several organizations that offer summer teen missions programs:

YOUTH WITH A MISSION

7085 Battlecreek Rd. SE
Salem, OR 97301
503-364-3837

TEEN MANIA

P.O. Box 700721
Tulsa, OK 74170-0721
1-800-299-8336

ROYAL SERVANTS

5517 Warwick Place
Minneapolis, MN 55436
612-823-4050

BIG WORLD VENTURES

P.O. Box 70323
Tulsa, OK 74170-3203
1-800-599-8778

International Union of Gospel Missions

1045 Swift Street

Kansas City, MO 64116

(Ask for the short-term missions directory. You can also contact them at http.//www.IUGM.org/sumr-dir.html)

Mercy Ships International

P.O. Box 2020

Lindale, TX 75771-7447

1-800-772-7447

Project Serve

Youth for Christ, U.S.A.

P.O. Box 228822

Denver, CO 80222

303-843-9000

Teen Missions

885 East Hall Road

Merritt Island, FL 32953-8443

407-453-0350

Teen World Outreach

7245 College Street

Lima, NY 14485

716-582-2790

JANZ TEAM

2121 Henderson Highway

Winnipeg, Manitoba

R2G 1P8

Canada

204-334-0055

60 ASK God if He wants you to be a missionary.

If you think bush rats and bugs are what missions are all about, you're in for a big surprise.

Here's Linda's story:

His name was John, and he was soooo cute! Tall, broad-shouldered, dark brown eyes with lashes to kill for and a bass voice that made my heart melt. He was just as good on the inside, too. Great sense of humor, sensitive, committed Christian—he was everyone's friend—and just being around him made me feel good.

He had only one flaw, but it was a major one. He had a "call" to be a missionary.

What a downer for this gorgeous, gifted, talented guy to bury himself in a jungle somewhere, never to be seen or heard from again! There was no way I was going to sacrifice *my* life and *my* dreams by being a missionary. *Forget about falling in love with HIM,* I thought to myself.

WAY BACK WHEN . . .

I hadn't always felt that way about being a missionary. In fact, I grew up in a godly home where missionaries were considered to be "top of the line" Christians. **When missionaries came to my church** and showed their slides, I was always touched by the faces I saw and the words I heard. As the slides flashed past, I usually sat in our darkened church and cried, wondering silently if God wanted me to be a missionary.

By the time I got to junior high, though, I tried to ignore those feelings, because by then I had a much better understanding of what those missionaries did. They didn't just travel around showing neat pictures—they had to go to far-away places to take those photos—places that had huge, disgusting bugs and poisonous snakes. Places where people dressed weird and spoke foreign languages and preferred monkey stew to Big Macs.

I knew this was not what I wanted to do with my life! I'd given my heart to Jesus when I was in first grade, and I wanted to do what God wanted me to do—just not on the mission field.

I figured He was probably testing me like He did with Abraham and Isaac—you know, just to see if I was willing. But I didn't want to say yes . . . in case He was serious.

EXCUSES 101

I had plenty of valid arguments. I didn't play the piano, so how could I win any souls if I couldn't plunk out "Just as I Am" for the invitation? And I'd definitely be too homesick to do any evangelism, because I really, *really*, REALLY loved my family.

In fact, I knew **lots of my friends** who were not getting along with their parents, so I suggested to the Lord that He call one of them. Of course, the best zinger of all was "There are so many people right here in America who need you, God, so why go somewhere else?" (That was my favorite because it sounded so spiritual.)

The bottom line? I didn't want to commit myself to something I knew I could never bring myself to do. I was so afraid of failing, so afraid of my inadequacies, so afraid that my life would be ruined and my hopes and dreams would go down the tubes, that I couldn't even talk to God about it. I wish I had been wise enough to *admit* my weaknesses and fears to the Lord and ask Him to change them, instead of using them as excuses to avoid saying yes.

You see, I never really said no, because I certainly would never say that to God! Instead, I just stalled, avoided, and ignored. But it kept coming up. It was always there. Just when I'd be having a great time spiritually, up it would come—this missionary thing—and I'd shut myself off from God rather than deal with it.

PERFECT PLANS

Finally, one night when I was a junior in high school, I lay in bed thinking about my future. I had it all planned. **I'd go to a Christian college and meet a great Christian guy** (someone just like John only without THE CALL). We'd get married, move back to my hometown, I'd teach for a while, and then we'd have children who could grow up surrounded by their loving extended family.

We'd go to church faithfully and be strong, supportive laymen (just as my family had been for three generations), and everything would be PERFECT.

Then the Lord spoke to my heart and said, "Yes, Linda, but you know that I want you to be a missionary." I somehow knew in that moment that the time had come to make a decision.

There wasn't anything wrong with my picture—not one thing sinful about what I wanted to do with my life—EXCEPT that it wasn't what God wanted.

In my darkened bedroom, I felt God's presence. He was *extremely* close. I heard Him say, "I will never force you to do this, Linda, but you must understand that if you choose your way over mine, at all the moments in your 'perfect' future that bring you great happiness, you will say to yourself, 'Yes, but I wonder what *might have been* if I had done what God wanted me to do.'"

I knew then that **I could never be content with second best.** I grabbed my Bible off the nightstand, opened it, glanced down and read these words from Matthew 10 that I had already underlined:

"If you love your father and mother more than you love me, you are not worthy of being mine; or if you love your son or daughter more than me, you are not worthy of being mine. If you refuse to take up your cross and follow me, you are not worthy of being mine.

"If you cling to your life, you will lose it; but if you give it up for me, you will save it" (vv. 37–38, TLB).

I knew that those were God's words to me. So I finally . . . *finally* said YES to Him.

CHANGE OF HEART

Have you ever read the Dr. Seuss book *Green Eggs and Ham?* Remember good old Sam-I-Am, who does his best to convince his friend to try green eggs and ham? **His pal isn't as stupid as he looks,** though, and refuses, knowing without having actually tasted them that he'd hate them.

But Sam-I-Am is very persistent. So finally, just to get Sam off his back, his buddy agrees to try them. We all know that he discovers, much to his surprise, that he actually *loves* green eggs and ham.

Well, that pretty much describes how I feel today. After all those years of resisting because I thought I knew what was best for me, I have discovered that saying yes to God was the smartest thing I ever did! I absolutely *love* being a missionary and wouldn't trade places with anyone. How thankful I am that God didn't give up on me and say, "Fine. You don't want to go—I'll find someone who does!"

Through the years, I've learned that **God wants my happiness even more than I do.** And guess what? I even got to marry John! We have three great kids, have traveled all over the world, lived in the Caribbean and Africa, and we have wonderful friends of many different nationalities.

Best of all, though, I've had the privilege of taking the gospel to those who have never heard it before and have seen people's lives transformed by the power of God!

WANTING GOD'S WILL

Most missionaries I've met always wanted to be missionaries, so they never struggled over their call. I *have* met a surprising number of people over the years, though, who have told me that God called them when they were young, but they chose another path instead and have always regretted it.

Esther 4:14 tells us that God will get His work done with or without you, but if you don't do what He asks, YOU will be the loser. So, in the words of a missionary friend of mine, "If God is calling *you* to be a missionary, **cancel the pity party and start the celebration!"**

Linda Seaman and her husband, John, have three children and are missionaries for the Church of the Nazarene in Cote d'Ivoire, West Africa. Her story, and the following "What About YOU?" piece by Susie Shellenberger, first appeared in the January 1996 issue of Brio *magazine.*

God doesn't call the prepared; He PREPARES the called.

WHAT ABOUT YOU?

by Susie Shellenberger

Is God calling *you* to be a missionary? Well, in a sense, He calls *all* of us. Some, He sends overseas. And others, He keeps at home. But wherever you live, and whatever your career will be, God still wants to use YOU as a light. **In order for you to shine effectively, you need to be growing spiritually.** Reading your Bible and praying on a daily basis are the two most important things you can do to strengthen your spiritual life. Some people call this devotions. You might call it your special time with the Lord. God isn't concerned about what it's called—He's just concerned that you do it.

Since spiritual growth is a *daily* activity, let's use the word "daily" as a recipe that you can use to grow closer to Jesus.

D: *Don't compromise.* With the Holy Spirit's help, you CAN say *no* to temptation. When you're pressured to cheat, claim His strength and say no. When you're tempted to watch something on TV or the VCR that's sexually suggestive, violent, or goes against God's standards in any way, refuse. **Living a life of no compromise doesn't mean you're perfect.** It *does* mean that you're committed 100 percent to the lordship of Jesus Christ.

A: *Ask for daily opportunities to share His love.* **You serve a God of a million possibilities.** He's more excited than you can imagine to impact others through you! When you ask Him to bring someone across your path that needs Him, He'll respond.

As soon as you've asked Him to do this, start thanking Him ahead of time! Then be on the lookout all day for that one person. And don't be afraid. God's not going to turn you into a religious fanatic or make you be someone you're not. He'll use your own personality—the special way He created you—to make a difference in someone's life.

I: *Realize the importance.* **You are very important to God, and He wants to do important things through you.** The faster you realize this, the sooner you'll become more confident in His desire to use you to make a difference. Never worry about what you can't do. God is the equipper. He'll never call you to do something without providing everything you need to do it. You see, God isn't concerned about your *ability*—He's concerned about your *availability*.

L: *Live the life.* **Did you know that the strongest testimony a missionary has is his or her lifestyle?** With that in mind, you can actually be a missionary right now! By living a Christlike lifestyle, you can be a life-sized Bible to the world around you.

Does this mean you always have to have a Scripture on your tongue? No. It *does* mean that your lifestyle should be so attractive that others want what they see. If you're always complaining and looking for the negative side of things, people won't want your attitude. Strive, instead, to wear a smile and encourage others. This kind of positive attitude is what magnetizes people to you.

Y: *Yes, Lord!* Let this be your life's motto. Be willing to say "Yes, Lord" to anything He asks of you, anytime, anywhere.

Heaven WON'T be boring.

Here's what you'll be doing:

- Playing golf, basketball, tennis, football, baseball . . . injury free!

- Talking with friends.

- Checking out all of the golden streets. (Maybe even some golden arches!)

- **Eating your favorite pizza** at huge banquets with Jesus and the twelve disciples.

- Singing like you've never sung before. (And *this* time you'll even *sound* good!)

- Basking in your favorite temperature.

- Sinking your toes into the best beaches or skiing the best mountains.

- Making the right choices. (Because when we see Jesus, we'll be just like Him. And He always makes the right choices.)

- Meeting people from history you've always wanted to meet (who were believers, of course).

- Shedding tears never again.

We already know we'll be doing *some* of these things. The other stuff? We're just guessing. But it could all happen.

This is for sure: It will be far different, more wonderful, never boring, and incredibly beautiful. It will truly be . . . HEAVEN!

63} LOVE others.

REALLY love others . . . not just the ones who love you back. That's not easy. **Put your love into action,** and love the kids at your school who are unlovable. Here's what God has to say about it:

"Little children, let us stop just *saying* we love people; let us *really* love them, and *show it* by our *actions*" (1 John 3:18, TLB).

If you **really love as Jesus loved,** you'll . . .

• find someone who's eating alone in the cafeteria and ask him/her to join you and your friends.

• start saying "hi" to the weirdo you pass in the hall every day between third and fourth period.

• stick up for those who are being put down by others.

• look for ways to **do something to help** (loan someone a dollar, offer a ride, help a friend study).

Get CONSISTENT with your devotional life.

How? Well, **there are several ways.** But instead of telling you ourselves, we'll let our *cwazee* friend Philip Wiebe give you *his* side.

HOW TO DO DEVOTIONS

As you may have already discovered, **doing devotions can be one of those good news/bad news things.** The *good* news is that devotions are really easy—they're just a way to get to know God better. The *bad* news is that devotions are really hard—they come in about 16 gazillion different versions, with more being discovered every day.

Where do you start? Well, I'll tell you . . . beats me! I have as much trouble with devotions as anyone. More, even. If you tried to map my devotional life, it would probably look like roller-coaster mania!

So maybe that qualifies me to give some advice on how *not* to do devotions:

1. **Stay away from gimmicks.** When you get right down to it, devotions have just two basic parts: (1) reading your Bible, and (2) praying. Sure, there's more to it than that, such as what to read, how to pray, and so on. But you need to watch out for devotional methods that add *so* much more, you forget what you're doing in the first place!

So please be wary of . . .

• study Bibles that have so many explanatory notes, you can't find any actual verses.

• pop music devotionals that try to dig deep spiritual meanings out of lyrics like "Do wa diddy diddy dum diddy do."

• Scripture trading cards packed with slabs of "spiritual fruit-flavored" bubble gum.

• devotional techniques that claim they can make you "a spiritual giant in three days or less!"

• anything with a picture of a clown and a name like "McBible."

In other words, avoid things that distract you from the main points: Bible reading and prayer. If you start your devotions with "Do wa diddy," you probably won't do diddly.

2. Don't think there's only one right way. "The only time to have devotions," someone told me back in high school, "is from 5 A.M. to 7 A.M."

So I started doing them from 5 A.M. to 7 A.M. Or more accurately, from 5 A.M. to 5:05 A.M., after which I'd be snoring facedown on my Bible.

The trouble was, (1) I wasn't a morning person, and (2) I'd rarely spent more than ten minutes at one time on devotions in my life. So how could I do devotions from 5 A.M. to 7 A.M. (except in my dreams)?

I couldn't. And neither can you if you're not ready for it, or it goes too strongly against your nature. In reality, there are as many different times, ways, and means to do devotions as there are people who do them. And that's a *lot*.

3. Don't get in over your head. When people see something missing in their lives, like exercise, they often try to dive in too deep. "I should start getting fit today," they say, "so I'll do an hour of aerobics, an hour on the bike, and an hour of weights!" After which they spend a year in trac-

tion.

It's the same with devotions. "I need to catch up," you might think to yourself, "so I'll read Genesis through Psalms today, and Proverbs through Revelation tomorrow!"

Sorry, can't be done. That's getting in over your

head. Devotions are like spiritual exercise—if you don't start out easy, you could hurt yourself. You don't want to make your devotional life such a huge pain that you end up avoiding it like the plague!

So now that you know some things *not* to do, what *should* you do? Like I said, read your Bible and pray. But how? Well, do whatever works! I can't say exactly what that is for you, but I can tell you some things that may inspire you to get going (or keep going):

1. *Devotions aren't a technique.* That's what messes up a lot of people—they take on devotions like they were studying for an SAT test. They think if they get hold of the right study guide, they'll ace that thing!

But **devotions aren't a technique; they're a way of life.** Maybe "devotions" should really be called "devotion." Reading our Bibles and praying are natural ways to make friends with and show devotion to a God who loves us more than anything.

2. *Devotions aren't a duty.* That's another thing that messes people up—thinking devotions are some kind of necessary sacrifice, like doing dishes or vacuuming the living room. But King David said in Psalm 51, "You do not delight in sacrifice, or I would bring it . . . the sacrifices of God are a broken spirit; a broken and contrite heart, O God, you will not despise" (vv. 16a, 17, NIV).

In other words, **God doesn't enjoy it much when we read and pray because we "have to."** He wants our hearts to be in it!

3. *Devotions are good for you.* Yeah, I know—when something's good for you it probably either tastes lousy or isn't any fun. And to be perfectly honest, **sometimes devotions aren't any fun either.** Sometimes they're tough! That's why Hebrews 4:12 says the Word of God is "living and active" and "sharper than any double-edged sword"—it "judges the thoughts and attitudes of the heart" (NIV). When you read your Bible and pray, you're probably going to find out things about your life that need to change!

But again, it's like exercise. It doesn't always feel great at the time, but it sure makes you feel better in the long run.

4. Devotions are a privilege. Some people think of devotions as spiritual homework—one of those nasty things you have to do to get in good with the Teacher. But Hebrews doesn't put it that way: " . . . since we have confidence to enter the Most Holy Place by the blood of Jesus . . . let us draw near to God with a sincere heart in full assurance of faith" (10:19, 22, NIV).

What an unbelievable privilege. Imagine! Getting to know the God of the universe! *Awesome.*

"Come near to God," James says, "and he will come near to you" (James 4:8a, NIV). That may not always be easy, but it sure is simple.

This article by Philip Wiebe will appear in a future issue of Brio *magazine.*

Run FAAAAAST.

From temptation, that is. **Many times we have it all backward.** We think, *OK, if I can face this without yielding to temptation, I'll be much stronger.*

Nowhere in the Bible does God tell us to deal with temptation by facing it. Anytime temptation is mentioned, He's telling us to run in the opposite direction *as fast as we can!*

So go ahead—memorize it (2 Timothy 2:22a):

"Run from anything that gives you the evil thoughts that young men [and women] often have, but stay close to anything that makes you want to do right" (TLB).

And while you're at it, go ahead and memorize THIS one, too:

"Oh, Timothy [insert your own name], you are God's man [or woman]. Run from all these evil things and work instead at what is right and good, learning to trust him and love others, and to be patient and gentle (1 Timothy 6:11, TLB).

Develop an ACCOUNTABILITY partner.

Though you make it to heaven by your own personal choice to follow Christ, you can't make it as a solo Christian.

Does that statement sound awfully definite? Extremely hard line?

Well, it is! **We've seen too many Christians try the solo route** only to fall flat on their faces. The reason (in case you didn't know) is Satan is just too powerful and too sneaky. He eats solo Christians for breakfast . . . and spits out the bones.

Ephesians, chapter 6 talks about the warfare believers are in, a warfare that doesn't involve flesh and blood, but one fought in the spiritual realm. We don't know for certain if our angels are doing hand-to-hand combat with demons, but we have learned from our own past that trying to live a godly life alone is like going up against a well-equipped warrior with a butter knife.

Every Christian needs an accountability partner.
This other person—a best friend, an older Christian, a parent, a youth leader—becomes a shepherd for your soul. Pastors can't do this for everyone, and neither can youth leaders. But God will bring someone into your life who is committed to your success as a believer.

What does an accountability partner provide? He or she can play a variety of different roles, such as

- **praying** for you every day.
- meeting with you weekly for Bible study and prayer.
- asking you the **tough questions**:

—How's your thought life been?

—How are you doing with your **girl/boyfriend?**

—Are you keeping your temper under control when a teacher treats you unfairly?

—What are you getting out of the Bible?

—What did you **hear the Lord** saying through your pastor at church last Sunday?

An accountability partner is a special kind of friend for you:

• Someone of the same sex. (This is mandatory!)

• Someone you can say anything to who won't blab it to others and will accept you unconditionally.

• Someone who will remind you of God's grace when you're too hard on yourself and God's forgiveness when you've blown it.

• **Someone who won't try to play God** in your life, but would rather point or push you toward God.

We're not saying a person like this grows on banana trees. But people like this ARE out there.

Pray that God will send someone like this into your life.

Relationships need time to develop to this point. They don't happen on a weekend sleepover.

When you find someone, give him or her permission to shine God's light in the darker corners of your life. If your partner steps over an edge or seems to be just giving you an opinion, don't run away; educate that person on what you need in an accountability partner.

And when a friend you trusted betrays that trust (and sadly, it happens), don't let that sour you on developing this type of friendship. **Start over,** be a little more cautious, then learn to trust again. **Remember, you're dealing with another fallible human being. People will make mistakes!**

If you want more information about this type of accountability relationship, talk to a parent, pastor, or youth leader. He or she will likely have something wise to say.

In case you're wondering, both of us have people in our lives who fulfill what we've talked about: Someone who has our best interests at heart, and someone we meet with on a regular basis. Even Christian authors need help!

67. Learn to ENJOY silence.

OK, this will make us sound like adults—and we *are* adults—but try not to take this the wrong way. This generation, more than any other since time began, is under a **constant barrage of noise and distractions** from the ever-growing media technology so affordable to most.

Computers, on-line services, portable CD players, video games, pay-per-view, Blockbuster, TV with eighty channels—all this and more—crowd into our air space and choke out any ability to let God speak.

Many teens do their homework with the radio or TV on. Some probably try to have a "quiet time" while listening to contemporary Christian music through their Walkmans.

All this media gadgetry has its place, but **unless you're able to sit in your room without anything on, it's going to be tough to hear God speak.** And if you're not listening to Him talk to you, you may not hear Him remind you how much He loves you. Then you might doubt His love . . . then you might *leave* His love. It happens.

There is more to be drawn from the depths of the Father while sitting with Him in silence than you can ever imagine. And unless you cultivate this habit during these years, you will have trained yourself incorrectly on how to survive as a follower of Jesus Christ.

68 Use your IMAGINATION.

God blessed us with creativity. Have fun with it! Here's one of my (Susie's) fun rainy-day creations.

DAYDREAMS

I'll always remember

Old Mother Hubbard's shoe

and my own special room

a place where rectangles are heard

and the alphabet smells pink

the door is left open

to old fiddlers with briar-patched faces

and anyone who's a friend of christopher robin's

in this magical world of miraculous mystery

solar logic begins with touch

mountains are created from cereal box explosions

and peter pan is mayor

papers shuffle

bells chime

the teacher continues

with equations

synonyms

and personification

but I dance with

Henry David Thoreau

and will forever remember

my own special place

with Old Mother Hubbard

69 Being a Christian means LOVING, not judging.

To see what we mean, check out this fiction story.

THE PHARISEE

"I smell brownies," Lisa said.

"Come on, Jerry," Dan said. "Let's wrap up this study on Matthew 23. All this stuff about Pharisees is intense—**my stomach's gonna digest itself if we don't eat soon!**"

"Hold it, gang." Our group leader held up his hand. "Whose turn is it to host next week's meeting?"

"Let's see," Dan said. "Tina's hosting this week. I did last week, and Staci the week before that, and Dan the week before that, and Michelle . . ."

I squirmed and caught Lisa's eye.

"It's my turn," Lisa spoke up.

"Okay," Jerry said. "Does everyone know where Lisa lives?"

"Yeah," Dan said. "Let's eat."

"**Wait a minute,**" Staci said. "Isn't it Julie's turn to host next week?"

The room grew quiet, then Dan noisily cleared his throat.

"I can't," I told Staci, forcing a light tone. "It'd be like inviting lambs into a wolves' den."

"I'm sorry," Staci said. "I didn't know."

"Let's eat!" Dan said.

"Wait!" Jerry said with a laugh. "First we pray, then we eat."

LET ME EXPLAIN

Staci came up to me while we were devouring the brownies. "I hope I didn't embarrass you, Julie."

"No problem," I said. "The other kids all know. I've shared before about my home situation during prayer time, but since you're new to the youth group, you probably haven't heard all the sordid details."

Staci took a swig of Coke. "I take it your parents aren't Christians."

"That's the understatement of the century," I answered with a short laugh. "My dad disappeared years ago, and **my mom has made a total wreck of her life.**"

"That's really a shame," Staci murmured.

"Yeah, the other kids gripe about how their parents are so old-fashioned and protective," I went on. "They should try having a mother who smokes like a chimney, drinks like a fish, and has a live-in boyfriend."

Staci's eyes grew wide. "Oh, how awful for you!"

"Well, I'm surviving," I said. "With the Lord's help, of course. If it weren't for Him, I'd probably be heading down the same path Mom's taken."

"Have you tried telling her about Jesus?" Staci asked.

"Oh, at least a thousand times," I said. **"It's like talking to a brick wall."**

Tears glistened Staci's eyes. "I'll pray for you."

"Thanks."

I had a bad taste in my mouth. On the outside, I'd developed a flippant attitude about my mother, but my nonchalance was just an act. I'd spent many hours pouring out my anger and sorrow to God.

HOME SWEET HOME

I got a ride back to our apartment complex with Michelle's parents. Michelle was moaning about the history test we both had tomorrow. I didn't have much to say. As usual, I dreaded going home.

Mom was sprawled on the sofa watching television. She stubbed out her cigarette in the overflowing ashtray and glanced up as I came in. "Well, if it isn't the saint," she remarked.

Well, if it isn't the sinner, I thought to myself.

"Smile," I told her, my voice edged with sarcasm. "God loves you."

I went into the kitchen where Tim—Mom's boyfriend—was rummaging in the fridge. We couldn't stand each other. Tim peeled the tab off his beer can and tossed it toward the garbage, missing as usual. Silently, I picked the tab off the floor and dropped it into the trash. Then I collected my schoolbooks and an apple and stalked into my bedroom.

Through the closed door, I heard Mom and Tim begin to argue. I listened long enough to conclude it wasn't about me, then I put a Christian tape in my cassette and clapped on my headphones. It was a typical evening of loving companionship in my family.

MORNING SUNSHINE

The next morning, Mom and I had a typical loving conversation.

I was doing some last-minute studying for my history test, and Mom was getting ready for work. There was a sudden crash in her bedroom, followed by a string of swearwords. I got up to investigate.

Mom was sponging up liquid makeup that dribbled across her dresser and onto the carpet. "I've cut myself," she told me.

"Go wash your hand. I'll clean this up."

I wiped up the rest of the makeup and threw out the broken bottle. Mom was struggling with a bandage.

"Here, I'll do that," I said, noticing how her hands trembled as I taped up her finger. "Why did Tim leave so early this morning?"

"None of your business," Mom said.

"It's my business that you set such a terrible example for me," I countered.

Mom ran a brush through her hair. The mirror reflected her bloodshot eyes and the tense set to her jaw. "I have a right to be happy."

"Happy!" I shouted. **"You'll never be happy living like you do."**

"Do you have to give me a sermon every time you open your mouth?" Mom said. "I'm sick of being told what to do by a pious little know-it-all."

"But, Mom, if you want real joy and peace, you should ask the Lord into your heart."

Mom lit a cigarette and blew smoke into my face. "Look," she said levelly. "When I want Jesus in my life, I'll let you know. In the meantime, just leave me alone. Do you understand? *Leave me alone!*"

"Certainly, Mother." I flung the words back at her.

STEERING CLEAR

I began going out of my way to avoid Mom and Tim. On school mornings, I stayed in my room until they both left for work. After school, I hurried home and grabbed something to eat before they got there. Then I went to my job at the

pizza parlor. After that, I went to youth group or studied at the library. On week-
ends, I went to church services and spent the night at Lisa's or Michelle's. I sel-
dom came home before 11 P.M., and then I went straight to bed.

Sometimes I heard Mom and Tim quarreling in the middle of the night, but
I never asked Mom about it. After all, **she'd told me to leave her alone,** and I had a
grim determination to obey her. It hurt to know she was so lost in sin that she
didn't even care about me. There was another kind of pain, too—an uneasy sen-
sation that the Lord wasn't entirely pleased with *me.*

DESPERATE

One afternoon, I came in after school and found Mom at home. She sat at
the kitchen table with a glass of something at her elbow and the ever-present ashtray. As I walked in, she wiped her eyes and blew her nose.

"What's wrong?" I said. **"Are you sick?"**

"Tim's gone." Mom made it sound as though the world had ended.

"You mean he's moved out?"

She nodded and burst into tears. "He met someone else."

"But, Mom," I said. **"That's what living together is like – no commitment."**

Mom squeezed her eyes shut and laid her hands over her ears. "Please,
please don't preach at me," she said with a moan.

I fell silent. Was that what I'd been doing—preaching *at* her?

"I love Tim," Mom choked out. "But he left me."

"I'm sorry," I said, and I was surprised that I meant it. **It tore me up
to see Mom like this.**

"Why should you care?" Mom put her head down on the table and sobbed.

"How can I go on without Tim?"

I opened my mouth to tell her how the Lord would never abandon her as Tim had. Then I shut it. If I said anything at that moment, I knew I'd be like the clanging cymbal the apostle Paul mentioned in 1 Corinthians. I had already *told* Mom the Good News many times. But I'd never really *shown* it.

All at once, **I realized I was like the Pharisees** Jesus spoke of in Matthew 23. Mom was the sinner in need of God's mercy, and I was the Pharisee, shunning the wrongdoer, treating her with contempt, giving her lectures, and wallowing in self-righteousness. I had some sins of my own to confess.

"When I want Jesus in my life, I'll let you know," Mom had said. I'd trust the Lord to show me the time and the words to use. For now, I prayed that His love and compassion would shine in my life.

I put my arms around my mother. "I care," I said softly. "I love you very much."

This story by Sara L. Smith first appeared in the July 1994 issue of Brio *magazine.*

Camp, Car Washes, Heaven, and Hell • 125

70. Angels are REAL.

When the Bible mentions something **over 300 times,** you get the hint there must be something important about it.

There are nearly 250 books currently in print on angels. Some are New Age, of course, but many—especially in Christian bookstores—come from a biblical viewpoint in explaining who angels are, what they do, how they do it, and why God created them. It is WAY beyond the scope of this book to go into the subject in much detail, but these passages should answer a few questions. If you want to know more, ask the clerk at your local Christian bookstore to point you to the best.

ANGELS CAN OCCASIONALLY BE SEEN.

"Do not forget to entertain strangers, for by so doing some people have entertained angels without knowing it" (Hebrews 13:2, NIV).

"But after he [Joseph] had considered this, an angel of the Lord appeared to him in a dream . . ." (Matthew 1:20, NIV).

ANGELS CAN BE COUNTERFEITED BY SATAN.

"For such men are false apostles, deceitful workmen, masquerading as apostles of Christ. And no wonder, for Satan himself masquerades as an angel of light" (2 Corinthians 11:13–14, NIV).

ANGELS PROTECT.

"For he will command his angels concerning you to guard you in all your ways; they will lift you up in their hands, so that you will not strike your foot against a stone" (Psalm 91:11–12, NIV).

"See that you do not look down on one of these little ones. For I tell you that their angels in heaven always see the face of my Father in heaven" (Matthew 18:10).

ANGELS SHOULDN'T BE WORSHIPED.

"Do not let anyone who delights in false humility and the worship of angels disqualify you for the prize. Such a person goes into great detail about what he has seen, and his unspiritual mind puffs him up with idle notions (Colossians 2:18, NIV).

THEY AREN'T AS IMPORTANT AS JESUS.

"So he [Jesus] became as much superior to the angels as the name he has inherited is superior to theirs. For to which of the angels did God ever say, 'You are my Son; today I have become your Father'?" (Hebrews 1:4–5, NIV).

71 } Do ONE thing well.

It seems there're a million different ways to serve Christ by serving people. In many churches, each week brings another chance to donate money to well-deserved projects or give your time to teaching Sunday school, serving in soup kitchens in the inner city, pounding nails in Haiti, fixing up an elderly person's yard, etc.

When you're young, you should try as many opportunities to serve as your schedule allows. **Do not let a month go by without doing something to serve another person.** But as you mature, you'll see there are more things to do than you have time for. You've probably noticed this in your parents' lives. They are called at home or challenged in church to serve on a weekly basis. Hopefully they've learned the true secret of success: saying no.

The key to God's blessing as you serve isn't saying yes to every opportunity that comes your way. **Trying to do it all will only burn you out,** your family will get tired of you always being gone, and you likely won't feel the joy in serving that it should bring.

To know the joy, to know you have God's blessing means that eventually you'll have to come to this conclusion: **God wants you to do one thing well.** He's given you many spiritual gifts and natural abilities for a reason—to serve expertly and with confidence. He also expects you to use those gifts wisely and **focus your time and energies on developing the one (or ones) you're best at.**

It could be in music, in teaching, in making sandwiches, in befriending the unlovely, in working with the blind or deaf or mentally handicapped, in phone calls, in leadership, in typing . . . the areas of service are endless. And so will be the chances to serve.

Ask God for a servant's heart, then volunteer to serve when needed.

Spend your life in giving.

Do one thing well.

And you will know the true joys of why God didn't take us to heaven when we were first saved. He wants us to experience the blessing of *being a blessing* to others. Just like Jesus.

72} WEAR your armor.

In fact, **don't even think about leaving home without it.** For a basic armor refresher course, check out what you should be wearing. It's all in the Basic Armor Catalog found in Ephesians 6:10–17 (TLB).

"Last of all I want to remind you that your strength must come from the Lord's mighty power within you. Put on all of God's armor so that you will be able to stand safe against all strategies and tricks of Satan. For we are not fighting against people made of flesh and blood, but against persons without bodies—the evil rulers of the unseen world, those mighty satanic beings and great evil princes of darkness who rule this world; and against huge numbers of wicked spirits in the spirit world.

"So **use every piece of God's armor to resist the enemy whenever he attacks,** and when it is all over, you will still be standing up.

"But to do this, you will need the strong belt of truth and the breastplate of God's approval.

"Wear shoes that are able to speed you on as you preach the Good News of peace with God. In every battle you will need faith as your shield to stop the fiery arrows aimed at you by Satan. And you will need the helmet of salvation and the sword of the Spirit—which is the Word of God."

Big sins are the end result of a BUNCH of smaller sins.

When you're in college, you won't all of a sudden decide to buy someone else's term paper unless you've built up a habit of cheating in school.

Someone probably won't have sex (or get pregnant) with their boyfriend/girlfriend unless they've moved from hugging to kissing, to kissing "sessions," to kissing and "exploring," to exploring and fondling on top of the clothes, to fondling underneath the clothes, etc. (You get the picture.) **It's a process** that can take weeks or months.

A person doesn't become an alcoholic by sipping their grandma's cooking sherry. They start by tasting beer at a friend's house, then later guzzling beer at a party because there are people they want to impress; then they get to actually liking the taste; then as they get older they want to drink every day because they like "how it relaxes them." Now we're talking about alcoholism.

A teenage girl who eats ice cream every Friday and Saturday night to make her feel better because she's not dating only occasionally becomes WAY overweight as a teen. **But soon she learns** that eating deadens the hurt. Then it becomes easier to deaden that hurt not with a *bowl* of ice cream, but a *quart* of Breyer's, washed down with a liter of Pepsi, six donuts, and a plate of brownies. Now we're talking about a serious eating disorder.

A guy won't become addicted to pornography by looking at the *Sports Illustrated* swimsuit issue once a year. But viewing almost naked bodies on a regular basis builds a desire to view completely naked bodies. And once your eyes have seen it all, it becomes easier to keep looking at different girls through the pages of whatever magazines are available. And that's how people as old as your dad (or grandpa) get trapped into a pornography or sex addiction. (Don't laugh at this one. It happens all the time to men who look nice on the outside, but are struggling BIG-TIME inside with an ugly habit that won't go away.)

What we call big sins actually start with minor compromises—stuff that initially

doesn't seem so bad, but puts you on a downward spiral. It often takes years before people will hit the bottom of that spiral staircase (and that will rarely happen in high school). But when they *do* walk off the last step, **they'll wonder how it ever started.**

Don't wonder anymore.

Now you know.

TRY fasting once in a while.

Jesus said, "When you fast . . ." (Matthew 6:16a).

Not *if*. WHEN.

Yet how often have you heard a message on fasting? How often do your own parents fast? **Just exactly what is fasting?** Going without ANY-THING for a whole day?

There are a variety of ways to fast. The most common is going without all food for a certain period of time. It can be a meal, two meals, a whole day, two days, a week . . . even longer. If you want to fast for more than a day, you first need to talk to your doctor (and parents) to make sure your system can handle it. Chemical and blood sugar balances are tricky. Fasts can also be done by going without food, but not without drinking juices. Of the various ways of fasting, none are more "biblical" than others. **The key is your intent and motives.**

You may be wondering why Jesus talked about fasting. Fasting is a way to focus your attention on God—to set aside your physical needs so you can really draw near to God. You're telling Him that you're serious about something. **It should never be to impress others.** In fact, the Bible says other people shouldn't even *know* you're fasting (see Matthew 6:16–17).

I (Greg) went on a two-day fast in college, water only. My spiritual life was going well, but I had some serious prayer requests. Plus, I felt there was more God could show me about himself through telling my body NO to something it kept screaming it wanted. I wrote down nine things I wanted God to accomplish during my fast. I double-checked them to make sure they weren't selfish requests. Each time a hunger pang hit, I prayed.

God answered all nine requests!

Since then, I've fasted when I wanted to show God I was serious about my desire to grow closer to Him, or to show Him my earnestness to have Him answer an unselfish prayer that needed immediate attention.

To repeat, fasting should be done *with a parent's permission*, without trumpets announcing what you're going to do, with good motives, and with a desire to **show God you're serious about seeing Him work in your life and others.** (And you shouldn't do it simply because someone else is putting pressure on you to fast. It should be your own personal decision.)

Fasting doesn't have to be just abstaining from food. It could be dangerous for some people to stop eating for a time (diabetics, people with bulimia, anorexia, or other eating disorders). Perhaps a fast that is even more helpful for teens is a *media fast*—going without TV, movies, video games, radio, or music for a few days, a week, a month. (Now, that's not going to hurt anybody!) Instead of spending that time to veg or be entertained, you read your Bible, pray, journal, read classic Christian books. In short, **concentrate on your inner life** instead of allowing yourself to be exposed to the constant distractions the world throws your way.

Under the RIGHT circumstances and in the RIGHT way, we urge you to consider fasting (from anything that keeps you from drawing close to God) on a consistent or semiconsistent basis. It WILL DO wonders for your spiritual life.

Make SURE you have camp memories to look back on.

Whether you go with friends or by yourself, **don't let your teenage years slip by** without hitting one or more week-long summer camps. Whether it's run by your denomination or a local youth organization like Campus Life or Young Life, more can happen spiritually during one week of camp than sometimes occurs in an entire year!

Why?

• Lifetime friendships are formed.

•You have time to put aside all of the media clutter and worries that fog your brain.

•God speaks to you, not only through the caring adults—the leaders, counselors, speakers—and through the program, but very often through the beauty of the camp itself.

Save money. Raise the money. Wash LOTS of cars! Do whatever you have to in order to go.

And take lots of pictures. (If you don't have a camera, get a friend to take some!)

You won't regret it!

Car washes are actually a pretty GOOD way to earn money!

So when your youth leader announces this annual event, try not to think about standing on your feet all day with the hot sun blistering your face or **getting soaked to the bone** or developing those ugly calluses on your hands from working so hard or the fact that **your back is screaming** for a chiropractor from being bent over the hood for eight hours.

Strive, instead, to **see the positive side.** After all, where else can you wear those cut-offs Mom says are too tacky for public, or show up in your fifth-grade softball jersey? No place other than a car wash will allow you to get wet, drive someone else's car, wear hideous clothing, and get paid for it!

But if your efforts to think positively fail, try to think *spiritually.*

• See if you can remember any of the Sunday school songs you learned as a child. **Try them out** on your customers, and see if anyone behind the wheel can sing along *with* you.

• If you haven't been baptized yet, approach your youth leader about a group event. You've got the water, right?

OK, we're kidding about the above suggestions. Baptism is actually something very sacred and an exciting testimony to those watching. But the bottom line is **you really can make some fast bucks** in a car wash if you choose the right location, publicize it well, and have enough teens working to handle the business. So when your youth leader announces the next car wash, get excited. Really excited. Or at least *act* like it.

Think about what REAL love is and how God showed it.

Sadly, there's a lot of stuff going on in the world that tries to pass for love:

•Two actors on screen pretending to be passionate (in front of cameras and probably a hundred people on the set watching).

•Musicians who say they "love" their fans. (*"And don't forget to go by the product table after the show and buy a black-and-white photo for $5 and a T-shirt for $29!"*)

•Moms and dads who have deserted their families, yet call and tell their kids they love them, while rarely making the effort to spend time with them.

You get the picture.

Love isn't sex.

Love isn't appreciation for what others can do for you.

Love isn't words.

Don't be fooled by the word LOVE. And don't try to fool others by using the word casually.

Real love isn't a fleeting feeling; it's commitment, attention, sacrifice, unselfishness, and . . . action. Love is a verb.

Real love is the God of the universe, the Creator of all that is seen and unseen, not zapping us into eternity alone, totally separated from Him.

Real love is this same God devising a way to reclaim His creation by becoming one of us . . . living among us . . . then in abject humility suffering on a cross to take away the penalty of our sin. Jesus, who knew no sin, took OUR SINS for us, that we might be clean and pure in God's sight.

"For God took the sinless Christ and poured into him our sins. Then, in exchange, he poured God's goodness into us!" (2 Corinthians 5:21, TLB).

Jesus did it willingly.

He did it knowing that many would not accept this indescribable gift and would choose to continue to trample His love under their feet.

He did it because He knew what real love was . . . sacrifice, attention, commitment, unselfishness . . . *action!*

You now know the extent of real love. **Don't ever be fooled by cheap substitutes.**